Happily Even After

By

Katherine Marie

Turtle Publishing

Turtle Publishing

Turtle Publishing Company ~ Jacksonville, Florida

~ *Dedication* ~

This book is dedicated to those brave enough to share their *Happily Even After* story with me, proof that fairy tales do exist.

People who honestly share difficult memories help future generations become stronger and more successful, and I applaud their courage. Those who hold fast to their commitment, when Happily Ever After looks different than originally planned, are my heroes. Instead of riding into the sunset, they stood together as life fell apart around them, redefining the fairy tale.

Thank you, to my family and friends who have encouraged me to take a step of faith and pen my own story of failure, struggle and hope in the search for my very own fairy tale. You are loved and I am blessed.

Finally, thank you, *Mr. Kind Regards* for believing in me, inspiring me, and pushing me every step of the way to follow my heart. *Happily Even After* was only a dream, until he helped make it a reality.

Thank you all from the bottom of my heart.

~ Forward ~

Richard Marks, PhD, LPC

There are many great books written from a first person perspective. But I have found it rare when an author shares not just what they learned from their life journey but their thoughts and feelings, joys and sorrows, regrets and rewards. Such is this wonderful work by Kathie.

I have known Kathie for many years. I knew some of her life journey but not all. When she asked me to read her book, I was honored. However, when I finally started to sit down and read it I found myself staying up later in the evening to keep reading.

As I read, I pictured her and I sitting down at a coffee table and I was listening to her tell her story. My thoughts turned to her openness, vulnerability, and how one could identify her need to share her journey not just as a part of her own healing, but greatly motivated to steer others away who might seek to walk the same path she did.

There is a Chinese proverb that says, *"If you want to know where a road goes, ask those that are coming back from it."* Such is this work.

As a professional counselor, speaker, and minister, I have heard thousands of these stories in my counseling office and seminars across North America. I have seen the hurt, pain, disappointments, anger, fear, and poor choices such have made. Kathie was no different.

What makes this work so unique is that she invites the reader, not just into her life, but her very soul. Kathie informs the reader that as long as one's soul remains wounded and disintegrated, poor life choices remain.

When Scripture states that we are to love our neighbors as ourselves it means it. Our ability to find a healthy and mature self-love and self-respect allows for healthy and mature life and life choices.

And of course, Kathie brings us to the Cross. For it is there where we find our greatest value and sense of self.

I hope you find this journey through her eyes and heart a journey worth not just reading but growing from in your journey into wholeness and maturity. I for one was blessed and upon completion of the book, I have a greater understanding of my friend, her life, her values, her worth, her healing, and her calling to serve others.

This book is her first step in serving you.

Dr. & Mrs. Richard Marks, PhD, LPC

(Louella)

~ Table of Contents ~

~ "Have Courage and be kind.
Where there is kindness there is goodness,
and where there is goodness-
there is magic." ~
Disney's Cinderella

Chapter One

~ *A Cinderella Wanna-be* ~

It's one of the first love stories I read as a little girl. Cinderella. With child-like faith, salvation from my own little corner and my own little chair by my own Prince Charming was, not only possible, but was expected.

My one true love would carry a slipper with the power to save me from my ordinary life. The whole universe would magically conspire to escort me into the presence of my personal fairy tale.

I had been a *Cinderella Wannabe* since I could remember. I believed in the fairy tale, and only the wildest of dreams. People laughed as I talked about my castle in the *Land of Unicorns and Rainbows*. I *was* Cinderella, at least without the evil step-mom.

I loved the idea of birds singing at my window and little mice scurrying around whipping up the most beautiful ball gown a girl could imagine. Doesn't every princess need a fairy godmother to turn a pumpkin into a horse-drawn carriage delivering her to the party of her dreams?

What's not to love about a story that begins with *Once Upon A Time* and ends with *Happily Ever After*? I instantly fell in love with the idea but later realized it might not be real at all. When I was young, the fairy tale ended when two lovebirds riding off into the sunset on a white horse.

There's a *Once Upon A Time* for everyone. It just happens to be a riveting tale of realities...including deadlines, bills, sick kids and lots of tears. Unrealistic expectations blinded me to the joy hidden in those moments, and for a long time, it robbed my story of its happy ending.

I'm a hopeless romantic. I mostly still believe in fairy tales, because the alternative is too painful. The more I lived, the more I uncovered countless love stories that would dwarf Cinderella's, stories rarely told. Protected in secret places, deep in the hearts of those who found great love in the ordinary, sacred moments.

The fairy tales in this book are from real people, living real lives, experiencing real tragedies and triumphs. These tales begin with *Once Upon A Time* and end with what I call *Happily **Even** After*. These imperfect couples have opened their hearts revealing honest love stories, and *my* honest love story continues...

The magic lives in thrilling moments and painful ones, making both uniquely significant. I missed many of those moments for years. I ran to the next destination, begging time to hesitate, if only briefly, so I could hold on to the sweeter moments, only to be heartbroken when they didn't last forever.

Happiness shouldn't depend only on the high points in life. The sum total of every moment strung together, good with the bad, should create a beautiful chain of events making me the brave heroine of my own fairy tale.

I experienced one broken relationship after another. For years unrealistic expectations and disappointments slowly chipped away at my chance for a happily ever after. Sadly, a few couples have it in their grasp, but fail to recognize it. And some, like me, slowly lose hope that it exists at all.

Hearing these stories were the antidote to that. I found the courage to press forward with hope, knowing it *is* possible to share a lifetime with one man who can and will love me through thick and thin, for better or worse, for richer or poorer. If you've lost a love through divorce or death, your story isn't over. God makes all things new.

"See, I am doing a new thing! Now it springs up; do you not perceive it? I am making a way in the wilderness and streams in the wasteland." ~ Isaiah 43:19

Don't lose hope. It's never too late to live *Happily Even After*. The Cinderella story for me is yet to be found, but I remain committed daily to watching the story unfold. The possibilities lead me on a journey to find true love.

I remember it like it was yesterday...

"Maybe it's not about the Happily Ever After. Maybe it's about the story." ~ Unknown

Chapter Two

~ *Once Upon A Time* ~

It was a hot summer day. The beach was lined with seasoned tanners, and some not so tanned vacationers from the North. I presumed they were all here for the same reason, to see the edge of the world. It could be viewed particularly well from a strategic position atop the fishing pier at the north end of Florida's famous beaches. The sound of seagulls filled the air along with the fragrance of fresh coconut. It was a picture perfect day.

This spectacular backdrop plays host to many weddings. What better stage for a commitment ceremony, than one provided by God himself. Bright yellow hues from the sun illuminated the fresh blue sky as seagulls with outstretched wings hovered overhead like angels. As long as the sea breeze holds back the rain, nature creates a magical, romantic place one can afford on even the lowest budget.

I was reluctantly eavesdropping from my favorite spot in the sand, surrounded by great friends. Rylee, my granddaughter, had joined us for the day. She naturally lent a childlike innocence to everything around us. Still young enough to hold the magic of the Happily Ever After story, she stood mesmerized by the fairy tale wedding before us on the beach.

Magical and breathtaking, weddings were meant to echo God's great unconditional love. Though beautifully breathtaking, it wasn't so magical this time. It just made me anxious. What was going to happen to these two? Would they take their vows seriously year in and year out, or would disillusionment wear them away?

"How quaint." The cynical whisper abruptly rose from my beach towel. I didn't mean to share my innermost feelings, but these days they poured out unprovoked and splashed over everyone like the waves hitting the pier. My love for all things romantic drowned in that vast ocean years ago.

With the pain of a recent divorce still fresh, I watched the ceremony with intrigue. Steady wind blew through the bride's semi-curled locks. Layers of white chiffon danced around the bride as if celebrating her all by itself. Their smiles looked downright naïve. The joyful tears in his eyes said, "I will love you 'til the end of time." Her eyes full of fragile trust said, "Prince Charming, my faith rests in your capable hands."

It was so magical, but untested and I couldn't feel happy for this lucky couple. It would have been a betrayal of sorts to the new me. How quickly would those tears turn to ones of sorrow? How many disappointments would it take to erode that trust?

Why was I so cynical? I was always the hopeless romantic in this group. What happened? It had been a hard year. Weddings didn't bring about the same feelings I once had as I watched couples share vows and promises. Now, it seemed natural to believe everyone eventually reached the age when good times were gone forever.

I grew up in a generation where people courted, fell in love, made commitments, and joined hearts in a sea of white lace and chiffon. The mere thought of rain doomed the couple to an unlucky future. So, with a clear sky and clear intentions, couples exchanged vows in a church before God, family and closest friends.

They witnessed true love for one another and pledged to hold to their promises. They ate cake, tossed flowers, and danced the night away. Once revelers raised the last glass, made a toast and threw rice, the happy couple escaped to an island paradise, where they began their fairy tale life together.

Sounds perfect, right? Not a chance. Marriage is the hardest volunteer job many of us ever undertake. Perfection was not on the list of options.

Prince Charming and Cinderella are figments of someone's imagination. I built my fairy tale on pure fiction. The truth is far more productive when it comes to marriage. It was up to my parents to give me a heads up at least, wasn't it? They tried. I figured I was too smart for their words of wisdom.

I was an expert at love until I got married, and by then, it was too late. I didn't understand it was okay if my perfect dream turned out to be a little less than perfect. I had already taken the plunge with my high school sweetheart, Prince #1. Why wasn't I okay with a *little less than perfect*? Although painful, it was certainly no nightmare.

"You can't ask me to change who I am." He once told me. He sounded so sad. Why did I want to change him anyway? Why did I think I had the right to even ask him to? So, at 12 years and 8 months in, my fairy tale was nowhere to be found. It wasn't supposed to end before *death do us part*.

Let me start at the beginning.

~ *"A blank canvas has unlimited possibilities."* ~
unknown

Chapter Three

~ *Christmas King* ~

I'd seen him at school a thousand times. I hoped he'd notice, but his popularity left no openings for someone like me. He had all the titles: Christmas King, Sorority Mascot and Most Likely To Charm. I, of course, had standards. Prince Charming had to show undying love, serenade me with love songs, and share my life's calling in our fairy tale future together.

The Christmas King loved to serve others. He wore his smile and good attitude like a badge of honor. He was an active member of the men's chorus and stage band, and music was my passion. Practices after school became our dates. We sat side by side at the piano, edging closer with each page turn, even though my sweaty palms made it more difficult to stroke the keys.

He'd never even asked me out. Our chemistry was little more than a teenage crush. Until the day we ran into each other along the outside corridor of our high school. Without notice, he grabbed my face in both hands and kissed me abruptly on the lips. Caught off guard and completely smitten, chills ran down my spine and goose bumps covered my arms. In one single act of bravery, Prince Charming showed up and swept me away.

That year, my dad took a position with an international airline company, which meant spending summers on the other side of the world. We had just met, but my prince started pulling away. The distance felt like rejection and panic erupted in my heart.

I moved across the ocean to a city in the Middle East along the Red Sea. That first summer, the letters I sent him were met with no response. I assumed the worst and stopped writing in an attempt to protect myself from his rejection. I'd pictured a knight in shining armor willing to fight for our fairy tale across the miles, proving his love for me.

It was a long summer, and Prince Charming never did come. I was young and didn't need rescuing, but I was a hopeless romantic. He was supposed to fight for me to win my affections. Certainly he couldn't give up so easily. It wasn't meant to be, and I returned home alone, openhearted, but ready for the next chapter.

He remained a character in my story, but when the next summer came, I'd return to that land away from home without him, once again. It was sure to bring more rejection. I couldn't ask him to put his life on hold. If it's meant to be, it'll be. There was so much more to accomplish without clouding my mind with fairy tales.

I wanted to be prepared this time and forget the search. I believed God would send Prince Charming, when I was ready, and we would ride off into the sunset to find our mailbox with *Mr. & Mrs. Charming* stamped on it. I at least wanted the American Dream: 2.5 children, white picket fence, and a dog. Perfection.

Each night I asked God to protect me from the hardships of dating and break ups. I wanted to be spared the pain of rejection I witnessed in my girlfriends. Negative experiences, I learned later, were teaching points that would've helped me through life. God answered my prayers, and I traded all that potential wisdom for one piece of the larger puzzle of happiness.

That next summer, The Christmas King was waiting when I returned home, but with a different attitude this time. Our relationship was now worth the fight, to him, and I was ready to be his one and only.

He didn't make much money, so dates consisted of listening to Bread's Greatest Hits from the soft white Flokati rug in front of the stereo. We romanced in the dim light and soft music, and skipped over all the important questions in favor of that superficial high. Being together was the only thing that mattered, and we were inseparable.

We stayed on the phone for hours. When we weren't listening to each other breathe, we were planning our fairy tale future.

Destined to share one life, I quoted to my parents, *"What God has joined together, let not man separate."* I didn't want anyone to stand in the way of my plan, not even my parents. God created me, saved me, and knew every hair on my head. He must have sent this man to me, and I wasn't going to argue with Him.

It was a rare occasion when I was treated to a dinner out. But when that special night arrived, he planned it like a true Prince Charming. On a cool evening in 1980, we shared a steak dinner and afterward, made our way to a dock overlooking the river. After a few awkward moments, he got down on one knee to pop the question.

The handmade engagement ring was shaped like a rose caressing a .5 carat diamond. It was small, but held the greatest meaning. Someone wanted to spend eternity with me! I wanted to say yes, but all I could think was, *please don't let that ring fall through the cracks of this dock.* It was the most romantic night of my young life. Of course, I said yes.

We got married the year after I graduated from high school. On our wedding day, I heard our church pastor shout out with excitement, as I walked through the church doors, *There she is!* I wasn't sure whether to cry or to laugh.

There was no time for second-guessing. I kept walking slowly toward the man with whom I would spend the rest of my life. There was strength in his boyish smile, and I believed we could conquer anything together. Barely adults, innocent, and hopeful, we began living our own fairy tale.

The wedding was just as I had imagined as a little girl, flowers, friends, family, commitment, cake, and a sea of white lace and chiffon. It was a picture-perfect day, not a cloud in the sky. I stood beside my prince wearing ballet slippers instead of those made of glass, but I was full of hope. Our mothers cried, and our fathers were filled with pride. After exchanging circles of gold, representing our endless love for each other, we kissed and lead the way to a celebration in honor of *US*.

When the last dance was danced, we said our goodbyes and took off in a neon-green, 914 Porsche Convertible. My veil flowed behind me waving goodbye to our guests, and we drove off to begin our honeymoon together. After staying on the ocean for a night, we set sail to the Grand Bahamas, our expected island paradise.

Within three years, we were a family: husband, wife, and two children: one boy and one girl, just like I had hoped. Now complete, we purchased a three-bedroom, ranch style home in a neighborhood not far from where we both grew up. It was *Happily Ever After*, finally.

What could possibly go wrong with two people so in love starting out with so much hope? I thought we had it made, but knowing how to make it all work was a separate dragon to slay. We inherited a promised land full of giants and enemies and neither of us thought to bring along a sword.

We had no idea what we were doing. It all happened so fast. We thought we were ready for family life and all it entailed. Blindly, we struggled through all the lessons young love with two kids, a home, and a dog afforded. We focused our attention on our children and failed to remain connected to each other first.

We looked happy on the outside, but made some really poor decisions in those 12 years. I was blessed with two wonderful human beings who remain the best part of that marriage, and I prayed immunity over them against our poor decisions. I wish I knew then what I know now.

We made a promise to each other before God and witnesses to become a threefold chord that would not easily be broken. For our marriage to succeed, we needed to put God first, make decisions together about our life, our home, and our future, and remain faithful to each other above all else.

Perhaps we were just too immature to know what true unconditional love looked like. Being a wife and mother gave me value. My self-worth was wrapped up in my relationship with my Christmas King, however misplaced it was. Of course he let me down, any man would have. My value should have come from within. By the time we had arrived at this place in our journey, we were simply too tired to fight.

We said and did hurtful things we couldn't take back. Respect and love faded and selfishness invaded our happy home. Our resolve had been tested in many ways, but not in defending the covenant of our marriage. It was selfishness, and we simply didn't know how to fight this foe. The enemy convinced us there was too much water under the bridge.

We needed to find a mission, a cause and forget about the water under the bridge. Worthy causes were passing right in front of us all the time, but we were too self-focused to see it. "Sometimes when you get on a mission, all the 'stuff' goes away," my pastor said.

We tried, but it was too late. Our mission failed miserably, and we said goodbye 12 years and 8 months after our fairy tale began. Unfortunately, that heartache was only the beginning for me.

~ "The wise treat yesterday's problems as water under the bridge. The unwise will treat them as a place to build a dam." ~ unknown

Chapter Four

~ *Castles In The Sand* ~

Memories of past failure always filled my mind as I spent hours in the sand. I felt closer to God in this place, but watching others take that step was an un-welcome reminder. With every gust of healing salt air I felt His reassurance, I was not forgotten. He saw me and it was okay, and in time, I would be too.

By this time, the wedding crowd had dwindled to just the main characters. The photographer strategically placed loved ones together for wedding album photos to have and to hold from this day forward. It made me take a hard look at the whole idea of forever. Sadly, our photos outlast many of our covenants. If we only had the same commitment to our partners as ink has to paper.

There was still an innocent girl inside me, like Rylee, who believed in fairy tales. With this question on my mind, I joined my granddaughter down at the shoreline as she built her dream castle in the sand. I knew the wedding ceremony had sparked hope in her, and I was glad my failure hadn't changed her spirit.

Maybe that's why so many couples spare the world their real stories, despite the necessary lessons in them. The hope that one little girl or boy has deep inside is precious. God placed it there, right? I believe it is His hope that we all see a *Happily Even After* story here on earth.

My grand-daughter's frustration grew as she tried to build a sandcastle in the midst of the quickly approaching tide, and I was strangely encouraged. The idea that it *is* possible to fall completely apart, only to be rebuilt is refreshing. True love causes people to rebuild those dream castles over and over. Every time a wave smashes it and carries part of it back out to sea, one must start all over again.

The process of love never stops. I watched the water demolish all she took so much time and effort to build. It became so clear that that's what the elements do to a relationship. But, when two people create a loving and safe environment that says, *I accept you just as you are*, the fairy tale *is* possible.

In my marriage, I didn't realize we needed to build and rebuild along the way. It was important to make specific investments in our life together, like measuring the distance from the approaching waves, or factoring in high and low tides. We were supposed to help cultivate our value and relevance together, as opposed to apart.

Making decisions that affected each other should be done as a team. I was a mom and musician, giving most of my time to child rearing, and the church choir. Though honorable, was that increasing our value? He was a provider and inventor, spending his time working and on his next project. Also honorable, but was that making us more relevant? With every decision, we made our relationship *not* so valuable, and each other *not* so relevant.

As we left the beach that day, I noticed the last of the wedding party leaving as well. The wheels kept turning in my head. Had God positioned me there at that very moment to re-grow something inside that had died years ago? I had to understand what went wrong before I moved to the next stage of life, lest repeat the same mistakes.

Our only conclusion was we had grown as friends but not as husband and wife. When our marriage failed, I lost my friend, the father of my children, and the extended family I had grown to love. I felt selfish, reasoning my failure must have been my need for a *better* Prince, or perhaps better for *me*. It didn't occur to me that a man's armor could become a little worn and stained. I was supposed to help shine his armor, and in the process, clean off the smudges I'd put there myself.

The idea the right man would come ready-made was a lie. I thought I accidentally picked the box with missing pieces, and maybe I could return it for a full refund. I was wrong. The pieces I needed *were* there. I would have found them had I looked closely enough. With God and our commitment, we had everything we needed to make it work. I wasn't sure either of us had made the choice to *truly* commit sealing that covenant, and it was evident.

My marriage ended with a single signature. *Irreconcilable differences*, they called it. Hopelessness signed, sealed, and delivered. Dream castle demolished and swept out to sea. I cried for many nights, but had two small children counting on me. It wasn't their fault. They were too young to even understand. They needed me in strength and wholeness, to help them feel safe, even if I didn't feel very safe myself.

If home was where the heart is, I was homeless. My heart had been ripped out. My mom's home would become my refuge for the time being. That first fateful night I hid in her bathroom, wiping tears from my eyes in front of the mirror. I tried to hide my pain, but sadness was now my shadow. I couldn't escape it.

"This isn't me. I'm the happy, *glass is half full,* girl. So, what now?" I said to the girl staring back at me. "Divorce?" I questioned. "Not you! You said you would never even whisper the *D* word." I was looking reality in the eye. "I suppose you've got this all figured out." I said sarcastically to the woman in the mirror, sweat leaking from my forehead. It was really more of a question, and I didn't have an answer for it.

I looked intently at the reflection wondering what to do next. I never wanted to raise two children alone, take care of myself, and feel so lonely. My hopes and dreams started to fade. I found myself in this unwanted role as a single mom. Nothing like what I hoped for. I'll just bet it wasn't my parents' hope for their little girl, either. Was this the fairy tale I had been looking for?

The girl in the reflection barely resembled the one in the white dress who made those vows at the altar twelve years ago. Only the shell of the girl I use to be remained. I wanted to look away, but couldn't. Was I the same frightened and insecure little girl?

Feeling like a failure, I sat down on the floor and grabbed a nearby blanket. Like Linus, I felt comforted by one. It was my friend, and I needed one right then. I just wanted to hear someone say it wasn't true. I needed words that said I was worth something. At the same time, I wanted to be brave without them. How could I show the world the extraordinary inside this weak shell?

The words I craved eventually came through family and friends, but then I realized a critical truth: my need for them was actually a reminder of my need for Christ. He was the only *extraordinary* person in my life. No matter how I felt, I had access to the power of Christ who dwells in me. Perhaps I'd find my *Happily Even After* in Him. I knew I should at the very least be looking in that direction.

Everyone was counting on me to get it together. I eventually found my heart once again. I moved into a new season of life caring for myself, and two children. Mom's home rescued me that day, and would again.

I held on to my hope of being rescued one day by the one man who could repair my damage, and help me find what I had lost. Maybe I would see Prince Charming differently this time. I entered into that first relationship thinking all the flutters were enough to carry us both through to our *Happily Even After*. If I loved enough for both of us, what could go wrong?

"Relationships are like sand castles on the beach. However harsh the waves may be, it can always be rebuilt again and again." ~ Prabh

Chapter Five

~ Worth The Wait ~

I knew couples out there living the fairy tale. Even if things weren't perfect, it *was* possible, and that gave me hope. My cousins were great examples.

It was 1975 and Joseph Charles Speiser, Sr. (Joe) was 17. Despite his youthful confidence, Joe's world was fixing to be turned upside down.

Her name was Linda Marie Walker. Smitten, though five years her junior, and they began a lifelong friendship. Linda, being cautiously guarded, asked Joe, "What do you love about me?" Grinning ear to ear, he simply said, "Everything."

Joe, never having much of a family life, was drawn to hers. "I would wake up on Saturday morning to go outside and get the paper. Joe was there on the door-step, waiting," she said with a smile. "He loved being around our family. All we ever did was hang out together, which made for a great friendship." Whatever Linda was doing, Joe wanted to be right there with her just doing the simple things in life.

After graduating from a private Catholic High School, Joe joined the United States Army, and before heading to Fort Bragg for basic training professed his love for Linda. She liked him too, but after being let down one too many times before kept her silence. Previous Prince Charmings had been anything but, and that left Linda discouraged.

The baggage she carried from those experiences was too heavy, and too comfortable for her to release. Linda had only been in a couple of relationships, but they never seemed to work out. Fortunately, God's plan included healing Linda from the inside out, and meeting Joe would restore her hope.

Time passed and he was transferred to Fort Benning. She finally found the courage to tell him the truth. That was the foot in the door Joe needed. He wasted no time popping the question. Linda knew she wasn't truly ready, so sadly for Joe, her answer was *no*.

Joe was a patient man, and had other concerns. Serving as a PFC in the United States Army, was called away for a year tour of duty in the de-militarized zone in Korea. Not wanting to go alone without a wife, he gently said, "We should get married."

At first, Linda didn't take it seriously. With a chuckle, she responded, "Yea, right, sure!" Heartbroken, and out of options, Joe left for Korea where he served until called back home suddenly for his nephew's funeral. Taking advantage of the time away, Joe asked her to marry him once again.

He refused to give up on his princess. Linda said, "I like you. In fact, I like you a lot, but I'm not ready to get married." Linda knew in her heart Joe loved her. She felt safe with him. But being so far away, and without a way to communicate, she was afraid their love wouldn't last.

Joe wanted to prove to Linda, no matter how difficult, her fears were unfounded. He recorded cassette tapes and sent them regularly to stay in touch with her. "They were scratchy, but I could hear him clearly." Linda said. Joe secretly clung to the hope that it would gain her trust, and her love, but to Linda, they were merely sharing experiences.

During Joe's deployment in Korea, God worked on Linda's heart, forming the perfect princess Joe needed in life for the future. Her vision was hindered by a lack of faith, but God had better foresight than both of them.

When he returned home in the fall of 1978, he took one final risk and pledged undying love for his Cinderella, pleading, "Will you please marry me?"

Determined to do one more thing before answering that question, she said with a new confidence. "You'll have to take me to the church first." Willing to do whatever it took, Joe drove her to the church that night. Linda stepped inside, and asked him to wait there while she went down to pray. As she knelt on that burgundy velvet padded bench, she began.

"God. Aunt Robbie said if I would ask you for a sign, You would give it to me. I'm asking." If God gave her the sign she needed, even a small one, she knew she'd say yes. If He chose to stay silent, she would get up from her bench and walk away from Joe forever.

At that moment, in the quiet of that sacred place where God and human hearts collide, the sign came. Joe walked to the front of the church, knelt there next to her, and prayed while holding back tears. She turned and said, "Yes, I'll marry you." And on that cold November night, their *Once Upon A Time* began.

Like a whirlwind, the December 10th deadline was quickly approaching. Joe grabbed two close friends and two family members and headed to Georgia for the nuptials before Linda could change her mind. Joe, in his haste, forgot it was Sunday and the courthouse was closed.

Though temporarily disappointed, they tried again on Monday, only to discover the courthouse didn't accept checks and Joe was without cash. "I'll be right back." Joe said to Linda. She couldn't help but wonder if she had made a big mistake, but in a flash he was back with cash in hand.

"You don't have to worry. I sold my Goose Gun. Now we can get married without any hitches!" he exclaimed. Joe had no trouble sorting out his priorities, which impressed Linda. Prince Charming was willing to do anything to sweep his Cinderella off her feet, even if it meant selling his precious gun.

Now Tuesday, with the marriage license in hand, Joe and Linda went to see the judge, who apparently wasn't there on Tuesdays.

Joe and Linda were going to conquer this giant together, no matter what. Out of options, but not out of hope, because there was another courthouse in the next county.

Joe could sense Linda's reservations returning, but couldn't bear the thought of losing her, so he immediately drove to Woodbine, Ga. Finally they stood before a judge, hand in hand, to pledge their commitment to each other. Just then, the judge's phone rang. "What now?" Joe shouted. They couldn't believe their eyes, and shared a nervous chuckle as the judge answered the call in the middle of their wedding.

The judge proclaimed them husband and wife, but not before jotting down the grocery list his wife recited over the phone. Linda knew if the enemy of love was trying this hard to keep them apart, they must be in store for something great.

"This time, we got things accomplished!" Joe told their families. They had six wonderful fairy tale days together before Joe shipped off to Ft. Bliss, and three and a half months later, Linda joined him in their new life together.

Linda's solo flight to El Paso was her first. Once she arrived, she sat down to talk to her new husband, quickly realizing how little they really knew about each other. Linda wanted to hop on the next flight home to the safety of all she'd known, but something about Joe and his strength convinced her to stay. Little did she know, the ride of her life was just beginning.

She moved into his apartment, quickly became pregnant, and just as quickly miscarried. Discouragement seemed to be around every corner, but their new home held the peace Linda sought. "It was the only house on Briggs Army Airfield with a tree," Linda remembers. She hoped it was a sign of new beginnings.

Linda settled in and made a life with her new husband. "It just felt right." She said. In no time at all, Linda became pregnant again. It was great news, but Joe's duties soon changed to a daunting assignment in Germany.

Linda wanted to be with her husband throughout the journey, but the doctor wouldn't allow her to travel overseas. Heartbroken,

Linda returned home to Jacksonville to be with her family. "I never felt more alone or lonely," Linda remembers.

When Linda got married, she never pictured herself pregnant, living several states away from home, married to a man she barely knew. Pregnant again, facing a mountain of discouragement and back in Jacksonville alone, Linda wondered when life with this man would finally be enjoyable.

Joe was never more in love with his Princess, determined to make a life for them once responsibilities to his country were fulfilled. Linda was equally determined to stay faithful in this temporary season of solitude. In the fall of the next year, with a new job, they purchased their first home, and a baby girl, Jessica Renee, arrived.

Like all good roller coasters, this incredible ride was full of twists and turns, some nauseating. During the week of Christmas, Joey barely two years old was diagnosed with type 1 diabetes, *Diabetes Mellitus.* It was hereditary, and usually skips a generation. Joe, at the age of 5, witnessed his mother's passing from this same terrible disease. She was only 26. It was an eerie reminder.

Discouragement found its way into their lives frequently, but they chose to dwell on the good instead of the bad, and never stayed discouraged for very long. The combined spirit of two unconditionally loving people carried them through the darkness.

Linda was delighted when Joe changed careers and took a local job at the City Sheriff's office. Linda says, "I felt like Cinderella, living in my castle with Prince Charming."

Linda's fairy tale, like mine, was complete. Prince Charming, two children, and plans for their first home were being drawn. It had to include extra space for her disabled mother and younger sister, Debra. That wasn't in Linda's original plan, but together they were going to make it work.

"No matter what we were doing, exploring or accomplishing, we were doing it together," Linda recalled. "That's the way we liked it."

They were truly best friends, and she was determined to keep it that way. With a background in nursing, Linda knew how difficult it would be to care for two more people. But, Joe had a huge heart, and loved Linda's family. "I didn't have a choice," Linda recalled. "Joe said, this was why we're buying the house, and wouldn't take no for an answer," Linda said. "I figured I'd know how to handle it, no matter what, and did with Joe's help."

She followed her heart respecting Joe's decision, and opened her home. Admitting things weren't easy, Linda looked for perfect joy everywhere. "I cried the whole time the house was being built." Linda said. But she fell more in love with her Prince Charming seeing his compassion. She felt blessed to care for her mother until her peaceful passing in that very home several years later.

Joe had always been a very capable and articulate man. From the Army, and the Florida Department of Agriculture to the City of Jacksonville, he generously gave his time and talents. He was either busy at work, rebuilding a friend's computer, or tinkering with a ham radio. "There was nothing Joe couldn't or wouldn't do for a friend or family member," Linda remembers.

He was meticulous about it. But, something changed. His steps became unsure, causing occasional falls and had trouble putting words together. At other times, not making sense of things. It was very disturbing to Joe and Linda, and the roller coaster sped out of control.

The same diagnosis came from the neurologist to the neurosurgeon, and various specialist. But, what was misdiagnosed as a brain tumor was actually stage four Glioblastoma cancer. Joe's only option was chemotherapy.

Linda knew what lay ahead with the cost of cancer treatments, both physical and emotional. She would have to dig deep to find enough strength for both of them.

As they walked further down this path, she watched him stumble and fall, struggle for words, and fail at things previously mastered. It was overwhelming. 30 days of radiation, five days a week for six weeks with oral chemo meds, and still they saw no sign of progress. A tug-o-war with God was going on. Linda was a woman of **big** faith, and knew God would provide the strength to endure.

"We just decided to live every day of our bittersweet fairy tale to the fullest, thanking God for every second together." Linda recounted. "We always took a trip to the North Carolina Mountains in the fall, but that year we would never make the trip," Linda said.

On October 4, 2013, Joseph Charles Speiser passed from the bonds of the mundane into eternal life in the arms of his Savior, Christ the Lord. The service was 'standing room only' for a man who was loved by so many.

Family and friends filled the pews along with sisters from the *United Daughters of the Confederacy*, and uniformed brothers of the *Fraternal Order of Police,* and a handful of *Army soldiers*. It was a beautiful home-going service.

We listened to stories of happier times and laughed with our brother. Then, a reverence came over the room as we watched his fellow service men carefully folding the American Flag. Wiping tears from her face, and clutching this precious gift to her heart, she received a steady and deliberate salute in honor of Joe's service then bowed her head in prayer.

We filed quietly, one by one, out of the building, to experience a heart-wrenching, and well-deserved 21-gun salute. The shots rang out across the still air interrupting the silence, at least for a moment. "I could not have been more proud of my Prince Charming," Linda said with a tear.

"I will love Joe forever. There will never be anyone as good, loving and kind as he." Linda says of her Prince Charming. He carried her, walked with her, loved her and cherished, not only her, but her family as well.

That love continues to carry her through the seasons to come, living on in the hearts of those who loved him. Her enduring love for Joe has proven to him that it was definitely *Worth The Wait.*

Linda and Joe's life together may not seem like a fairy tale to an outsider, but it sure was to Linda. She can't talk about their life without tears of gratitude for the beautiful relationship they were able to share with the world. They were never embarrassed by it and everyone envied the love they had for each other.

I was determined now more than ever to find the one who would be worth the wait. However, it would take a little more than fairy dust to make my dream come true. I was now a full time businesswoman and mother.

Tired and afraid, I was too exhausted for the search. Prince Charming would have to be right in front of me to find him. I needed only to look up, and so I did.

~ *"If what's ahead scares you, and what's behind hurts you, then look above. God will guide you." ~*

Unknown

Chapter Six

~ *Tink's Rescue* ~

We met at church, Prince # 2 and I. We enjoyed singing together, first in the choir and then a trio. He was one of the most talented vocalists I'd ever heard. We became a popular option as wedding singers, but because so often associated as a couple, accepting those invitations seemed unfair to our spouses. After my divorce, it seemed even more so to his.

It was unheard of for a *single* woman to sing with a married man in a Baptist church, even for a wedding. It seemed my new *single* status piqued everyone's interest. Meeting up to sing love songs with someone else's husband wasn't all that acceptable either.

I remember our last wedding gig together. I was running late. I parked as close to the church as I could and ran through the halls to the basement where we were to meet for a quick run-through. As I turned the corner and came to the top of the stairs, I was met there with an outstretched hand.

Taking my hand in his, the panic of the moment melted away into the strength of his confidence. He led me carefully down each step, letting me know everything was fine. At that moment, and feeling rescued, a prince stood in his place, and I saw the armor shining from underneath his cummerbund. I must admit it wasn't a great way to begin a relationship.

"Consider what a great forest is set on fire by a small spark. ⁶ The tongue also is a fire, a world of evil among the parts of the body. It corrupts the whole body, sets the whole course of one's life on fire, and is itself set on fire by hell." James 3:5 ESV

It was a spark setting my world on fire in more ways than one. All I wanted to do was run. I left my home church and my singing behind, and with it, the thought of Prince Charming. Having been recently divorced, I wanted a change of scenery. Feeling like I was underneath a blanket of criticism and shame, I planned my escape. I never knew what *big* change was on the way.

I decided to put aside any thoughts of being the other half of anyone or anything, and focus on myself, and what I felt called to do.

I started leading a children's choir at the daughter church of the one I had attended as a teenager. The pastor and his wife, along with most of the musicians were people I had grown up with, and I felt safe once again. It wasn't where I thought I would be at this stage in my life, but at least I was no longer in the middle of the drama I had run from.

Seeing happy families there gave me hope. Most of my old friends from the youth group were now married with children and seemed happy. They were living their fairy tale. Why wasn't I?

My first attempt at Happily Ever After failed. I was floundering around in a sea of naïve romanticism. Save the date announcements reminded me that young girls still believed in that Happily Ever After fantasy, sort of like children believe in the tooth fairy or Santa Claus.

"I'll find that perfectly wrapped gift under the tree, the one meant for me, if I just believe." I thought. Overwhelmed with feelings of failure, I *did* stop believing. What was left for me? How could I have a Happily Ever After now?

In the wake of that divorce, I told myself marriage had been a mistake the first time. I made all kinds of excuses. They were as flimsy as a wet paper plate, but they worked magic on my self-esteem. I was too young to know what I was doing. I didn't know what true love meant, I thought.

A year went by, and as destiny would have it, my prince showed up again and brought hope with him this time. We had become *kindred spirits*, since he too had by now experienced divorce. We were traveling the same road. *Certainly that was the spark I was looking for*, I thought. I admit, I wanted a knight in shining armor, and in my loneliness and desperation, it seemed as if God had provided one.

I was a fighter, feisty with a dash of sass. He appropriately labeled me "Tink". In my failed efforts to be Cinderella, I settled for the equally famous little sprite. It was the fighter in me that wanted to take the next step, but it wasn't going to be easy. At least I had my magic fairy dust to rely on, right?

He toured and sang with a group in the late 70's and early 80's. Coincidentally, I'd auditioned for them as a teen but declined the invitation. After a dozen or more years, and two divorces between us, I received an invitation to join the group once again. This time I said yes, believing this must be a divine appointment, my destiny... serendipity.

There was a connection, and we immediately became close. After all, we had sung together on many occasions and knew each other well, at least on the surface. It seemed safer than dating. I was still trying to control the amount of rejection I was willing to experience, no matter how much wisdom may have been born out of it.

Rehearsals became our dates, along with recording sessions and performances. Common ground brought us closer to each other. Looking back now, I was taking the same path I had taken the first time around, completely unaware of it. I had traded the armor and white horse, for this spark I felt in my heart. We were both so desperate to be understood.

We had gotten divorced within a year and a half of each other. No matter how hard we tried to dispel the negative talk surrounding our union, it only added fuel to the fire. There was nothing we could do about it once the vows were said, so we clung to each other and faced it, head on.

The romance was overshadowed by baggage dragged around by second unions, the ones you try to forget about. No white lace and chiffon this time, just matching sweaters for the boys and dark green, velvet dresses for the girls. Everyone was standing unified, singing together as a family.

At least we looked blended, even if it was just for the camera. The church was tiny, but that didn't matter, it was closed to family and closest friends only, those who could show a sign of solidarity. Surrounding ourselves with people, who believed in us, was vital to our success.

We stood side by side against the world, and it bonded us together like superglue. We became *us*. I think the struggle itself got us through those first few years together as a blended family. He had 2 boys; a 3 and 5 year old, and I had two children of my own. This would either kill us or make us stronger, and for a while, it was the latter.

I've heard that seventy-five percent of all second marriages end in divorce because two families and their baggage collide. We had plenty of it to go around. The kids were all jockeying for their spot in the family lineup, while begging for alone time with each respective parent. We went from no middle child to having two at the same time.

It was my hardest battle to date. I had to love children who weren't mine and allow them to love me, *or not*, in their own time. Although support from ex-spouses would never come, he had to provide for and lead this family, baggage included. We were in it now, so our only choice was to move ahead with faith.

We found a home, and a church, and set out to find purpose together. Our kids depended on us to hold it together, and for years, we presented a powerfully united front. We showed the kids that it was now *Us* against the world, and *Us* included them. It made them feel safe. We were determined to beat negative statistics.

Lessons came quickly as we navigated child support payments, alternating vacations, and pick up and drop off times, without allowing angry emotions to surface. No matter how hard we tried to stop it, resentment seeped into our happy home, drop by drop. It was a struggle, at times, learning to love my new bonus boys, knowing they may never reciprocate.

What about *my* children? It was difficult for him to love my nine and ten year old as well due to the strong bond they already had with their own father. There were swim meets, and football games, piano lessons and chorus concerts, overlapping each other occasionally, but we did what we had to do.

We learned the hard way that it was best to follow the rules, and keep the peace for the sake of the children. We stood strong against the naysayers and showed them that a happy blended family *was* possible.

I was sure, I'd married my soul mate this time, so, what could go wrong? I believed that everything about him to the core was divinely matched with me, as if the creator of the universe fit us perfectly in every way. It made all other connections feel empty or shallow.

Soul mates spent their lives in search of their counterpart, and when they found their match, they knew it to the core. I felt that way about him at the time. I've asked myself many times since, "What went wrong?" I thought we were living the dream.

"...your adversary, the devil, as a roaring lion, walketh about, seeking whom he may devour:" 1 Peter 5:8 KJV

The enemy doesn't sleep. He doesn't give up easily, and he knows our weakest places. He doesn't present himself in rags, snarling and growling with a red suit and a pitchfork. He sneaks in, quietly setting you up for failure. That enemy followed us, and started opening our baggage right in front of us.

Everyone carries a measure of baggage from the past. Sometimes it's stowed and locked away. The problem is, at some point, turbulence strikes and causes the baggage to tumble out and fall on everyone below. It leaves a mess, causing scars and entanglements that make a huge impact on our lives. It births resentments and hurts requiring a whole lot of love, compassion and attention. I thought we had mastered it.

It's downright tempting to make it work with someone kind enough to carry around our baggage for a while. Every girl wants someone to take charge of her baggage from the time it hits the carousel, and reaches home safely, to the time it's unpacked and put neatly away. Well, maybe 'neatly' was a little far-fetched but you get my point.

This Tink's baggage was simply too heavy for one man to carry. She had insecurities. She questioned, not only his love for her but also, her value as a wife. Feeling guilty for past mistakes, I failed to set effective boundaries for my first husband. He couldn't meet our expectations, financially or physically, leaving the kids questioning his love for them.

My apathy planted a seed of resentment in my rescuer. He became exhausted trying and simply gave up. I spent so much energy fighting dragons, to make the blended family healthy that I failed to consider making myself healthy.

I had never conquered the insecurity I felt from my past. I based my emotional security on how well I could keep the peace and please everyone, securing the *'Most Likely To Succeed'* award. It was not a great foundation to build a home on, and it fell. Castles built on sand last for a while, but sand shifts when the tide comes in, and I'd built mine too close to the waves.

I wasn't paying attention to the most important thing, and that was *Us*. My friend Dr. Richard Marks says when we get married, there is a whole new person created called, *Us* ~ **Marriage For Life** by Dr. Richard Marks. "If *Us* wins, we both win." Dr. Marks shared. "If *Us loses, we both lose.*" *Us,* was falling way behind. I wasn't listening to *Us*.

My husband communicated his concerns, his desire for me to make changes, but I rationalized. I didn't want to hurt my children by making demands on them, or their father, they were unable to fulfill. I was a people pleaser by nature, and showing grace to the father of my children, helped soften the guilt that kept me a victim.

I wasn't trying to be rebellious or disrespectful, although it felt that way to him. I believed it was the right thing to do. Mostly it made me feel better about myself for past mistakes.

It's easy for one or both partners to move through life selfishly, not paying attention to the other's needs, and if one of us is not happy, then *Us* is not happy. Mixed together with lots of miscommunication, it creates resentment. Left unchecked resentments turn into bitterness, and bitterness into contempt.

Contempt is the enemy of every relationship, and once it sets in, the chances for resolution are overwhelmingly low. Contempt can only be overcome by the unconditional love of God and true humility.

I began to believe life was unfair and was starting to become bitter about it. I hadn't reached the contempt stage yet, but nursed my bitterness until I forced myself into an emotional jail cell. This prison door was locked from the inside, but because it became so comfortable over time, I no longer looked for the key to let myself out.

My friends and family saw my pain and rooted for me to leave my isolation. My self-made dungeon only kept me from the things He had for me to accomplish. The key, within my reach, was waiting for me to learn I couldn't live a faithful or fruitful life confined within the walls of my guilt.

God provided a way out. I only had to take Him at His word. He was longing to spend time with me. He was ready to break every chain, and tear down every wall that stood between us. The *Lover of my soul* longed for an intimate relationship with me if I would take a step of faith, releasing my guilt to Him.

I no longer wanted to be defined by my mistakes. I was worth loving. *Us* was worth another try. I had forgiveness in my heart, but would never be given the opportunity to prove it. It was too late. We had already grown apart. "It takes two to make it work, but only one to kill it." Dr. Marks said.

We began to believe the enemy's lies. Forgiveness is out of reach, we said. We've hurt each other too much and simply can't move forward. We had fallen out of love, and directly into contempt. Ironically, quickly, and without much disagreement, we divided our belongings and checked the box that said irreconcilable differences parting ways.

To my knowledge, there is no such thing in God's plan. I had matured enough to see this now. Nothing is irreconcilable when God is the center, yet it's a common escape hatch for so many couples. It is always irreconcilable when one person refuses to stick it out at the expense of the union. I wondered why society had made it so easy. It takes longer to get a marriage license than it does to dismantle an entire family.

I wanted to try, but he truly didn't believe I could. There was no fight left in him. I'd begged God to save it over and over. I spent years thinking, if I just had enough faith, prayed more, fasted longer, worked harder, I would be healthy enough for both of us. No matter how hard I worked, I couldn't be his savior. I couldn't even save myself.

I wanted God to spare me this valley, but I found out the hard way, He doesn't always take the cup away. He didn't spare His own Son. God knew the only way to His perfect will was through that cup. I only trusted God when His solution came packaged the way I wanted.

I began idolizing my own ideals, twisting scriptures to make it fit my desires. I wanted God to fix it, put it all back together. Surely He wanted the same thing. It was an honorable request. But, God wanted me to want *His* will and not my own. He wanted me to find contentment even in the suffering.

It was a hurtful season, one of the lowest valleys in my journey, and I didn't want to be weakened by it. That would make me too human. I always heard all things were possible with God, but my experiences left me with little strength and even less bravery. I seemed to be facing impossible odds. My strength was limited to what little I could carry on my fragile shoulders. As for bravery, I only mustered enough for those who needed me to be.

Discouraged and alone, I was paralyzed. "This isn't what I signed up for!" I cried out to God many times. "This isn't the life I wanted." Why didn't God fix it all? Why didn't He exercise His sovereign will to save my marriage? This couldn't possibly be His will.

Where are you God? I already knew the answer to that question, even though I asked it over and over. I knew He was with me. I just wasn't willing to wait on His guidance. I felt abandoned, although I knew the bible said otherwise. I just wanted to be happy.

As I get older, time speeds up, and I rush to acquire all I desire, the things I thought made me happy. The opportunities were fading. Weeks, months, years went by, and I found myself standing alone, wearing no ball gown, no glass slippers, and certainly no pumpkin shaped carriage to take me anywhere worth being.

I made too many mistakes. Could I ever trust myself again? How was I supposed to live this life any other way? My picket fences were becoming huge walls of stone. How would I ever love again if I couldn't let the walls down around my heart? How would I ever be able to let someone love me if I couldn't even love myself? It would be hard to trust even a *good* man if I couldn't trust God.

I hated myself for doubting God, and loathed being afraid. There's just nothing quite like failure. It hurts from the inside out. I had already spent half of my life trying to shield myself from the pain of failure, because it ran into deep places I never knew I had.

I was afraid of love itself, particularly the idea of risking it all to find myself, once again, with a man whose love I doubted. I began to see a pattern. It is impossible to love without being hurt, and many times, hurt came by my own choices. I needed healing from wounds inflicted long ago, and never knew it, or admitted it.

For that brief moment in time I had the twinkle in my eye, the spark, but it had faded. No matter how bad I wanted things to work out, there was nothing I could do but trade my fairy tale for reality. You can't make someone love you when they don't. You can't affect a man's free will. God won't even do that. He sends us signs, and guides us with His Word, but ultimately, the choices are ours alone to make.

It became comforting to sit alone, as I did every night. I didn't mind being alone at this stage of the game. I'd watch movies and lose myself in someone else's drama, get swept away in its sad story, and then root for the happy ending. Movies were a temporary fix for my loneliness, but there simply weren't enough Hallmark movies to satisfy an all-nighter.

When I saw the movie *About Time,* this line stood out to me. *"No amount of time traveling in the world can make someone love you."* As a movie lover, I'm always amazed at God's way of seating me in lonely theatres where the most obvious lessons awaited. I always asked for signs, too. I asked Him to write His plan on the wall, or in the sky, but He used Dolby Digital Sound to get His point across, loud and clear.

The quote seemed oddly familiar, resonating deeply with me that night. The words comforted *and* saddened me. Something about them seemed hurtful while still healing. It was as if they possessed an incredible ability to lock me up and free me in the same moment. If love is forced, it ceases to be love and no one wants that choice taken away, not even Cinderella.

And we know that for those who love God all things work together for good, for those who are called according to his purpose." Romans 8:28 ESV

I made it out of the storm, yes. I knew God was true to His promises. I actually did trust God to work everything out, but not before I spent some time dwelling on the failure. The enemy likes it when we wallow in self-pity, and apparently I wasn't going to deny him his pleasure in mine.

Chapter Seven

~ *Pity Party* ~

Ultimately, I couldn't make my husband love me, and no amount of time was   going to change that. I felt pitiful, but the last thing I wanted was pity. In time, I hoped my story would encourage others. But for now, I was beginning the invitation list for my pity party. I was no charity case, and the thought of being anyone's third wheel wasn't appealing at all. I didn't want my children to say, *"We have to go to mom's, or she'll be alone."*

When things started to go wrong in my marriage, I threw enough pity parties to cover the entire family, and it had terrible repercussions. The more I felt sorry for myself, the less I had to give to the people I loved. It's an incredibly smart strategy on the enemy's part. Focusing on what I didn't have, robbed me of my joy. Being self-focused is a lonely proposition.

I was in un-familiar territory and felt sorry for myself, and ashamed. I've made so many mistakes. Was I not good enough, a quitter, or someone who just threw in the towel? Some people tried to show their love, but it always came out looking like pity. Some just looked away.

People have no idea what to say. It's not their fault. They judged me, others supported me, and others just avoided the subject altogether. One thing was for sure. I found out who my true friends were. They loved me right where I was.

I had my fairy tale planned out so perfectly, and it didn't look like this at all. I wanted to be carried away by love. I wanted to be overwhelmed with delirious passion. I didn't have a plan for when things didn't work out that way.

My mom's advice was always welcomed. She told me, "There was a time I prayed for God to give me answers. I cried out. What more do you want from me? He simply replied, *Persevere.* So that's what I did, and it's a continual process. Even if relationships fail, you don't stop persevering. Life is an uphill climb, not a leisurely stroll." She finished.

Mom was a praying woman, praying for us continuously. It was a habit that I respected. I felt the prayers, but in my solitude it was quiet, eerily quiet. Either way, the uphill climb had become steeper, and I would have to take that path alone. Mom couldn't fix this for me. No one could.

So I went back to my lonely corner, in my new-to-me home. Unfamiliar sounds kept me up at night, a scared little girl sitting on the edge of that lonely chair. Negative voices in my head said, *no one understands how you feel. No one cares.*

Satan has a way of alienating you from others. I began to believe that my suffering was unique to me. If he can get you by yourself, he has a better chance of defeating you, taking away hope. Believing no one had experienced this kind of hurt before, I wondered why life seemed so easy for some people, and why it was punishing me. What had I done to deserve this? I battled these questions as I sank deeper into my pity party.

I knew deep down that I wasn't the only one who experienced pain and suffering. Some struggles made mine seem small in comparison. I also knew that I wasn't alone, even if I felt lonely at times. Life still wasn't easy, but it wasn't easy for anyone. Once I could agree with that, I could begin to challenge myself to rise above its sorrows.

I truly believed helping others in need was the best form of therapy. It's difficult to be encouraging while in the midst of your own pain and suffering, but it is a sacrifice worth making. Things worth achieving come with a price tag. The sooner I learned that truth, the sooner I could begin paying the bill.

Bad things happen to perfectly good people. It's easier when those perfectly good people are others. I was certainly getting more than my share, I thought, but that would make me the victim again. It was time for me to play the victor in my own story. If I'm gonna have a *Happily Even After*, it's gonna be up to me. My circumstances don't control my happiness, I do.

I wasn't the only one to experience this kind of failure. I was in good company. All the successful people I knew had failed first. Every living, breathing creature shares this predicament. Successful people just get back up. I needed to get back up as well. With that thought *Happily Even After* felt attainable, but not before a few questions.

"Why me?" I asked. Ben Franklin said, **"Those things that hurt, instruct."** Trying to protect myself from learning things the hard way was my specialty for a long time. I had been under some intense instruction lately, and I made up my mind to find the meaning in all the pain.

I had fallen into depression, which was hard to admit. "Kathie, you are moderately depressed." My Dr. said. "Would you like me to prescribe something?"

I barked back at her, "I am **not** depressed, I am angry. I want to fix the problem, not medicate it." I said. I knew the problem was **me**. That would mean as a Christian, I had failed twice at marriage *and* at holding myself together too? I was supposed to be able to conquer anything as a child of God. My bible told me so.

For nothing is impossible with God." Luke 1:37

Depression is a very lonely place, but I was drawn to my bible, my journal and my knees. It was a healthy way to ride the emotional roller coaster I had boarded, although it still came crashing down uncontrollably at times. I wasn't prepared for how I might feel at any given moment. The panic attacks were something I never experienced before. I didn't understand it, because I usually had it all together.

Pity Party

Sometimes I wanted to be surrounded by people, but most of the time, I just felt like crawling in a hole. I didn't want to be in a crowd of people when my roller coaster came crashing down. I felt safer at the beach alone, reading, praying and listening to music, At least then I was free to cry without having to defend myself.

As unhealthy as it may seem, technology had become my antidepressant. I waited in anticipation for my next dose, which usually came as a text message from a friend. Often I would sit for hours with it in my lap, wishing and hoping someone was thinking about me. It was never all that odd to wake with it clutched in my grasp as if I was holding a winning lottery ticket.

I thought somehow words from a text might make sense of it all. Words can tear down or build up a person and I was looking for the building up kind. I used every resource at my disposal to find an antidote to my suffering. If Google could find it, videos, blogs, devotionals, song-lyrics, I was interested in it.

Almost daily, during the darkest hours of my life, words came. I felt so blessed to have friends and family who continued to pour out their love with words of encouragement. I will never forget the day I received a text from a friend asking if I was okay. "I miss being held and being loved," I responded. His reply was swift and unexpected. It gave me strength to take one more step out of the pit I was drowning in.

It read: *"You are being held. You are loved and He thought you were worth dying for, as it should be for the lover of your soul."* I was speechless, and anyone who knows me, knows that doesn't happen a lot. God sent me a special reminder, telling me whose I was, and who He is. There I found a certain measure of grace that exists only in the most special of places. God reserves special connections for those who can safely possess the grace shared within their boundaries.

Why was I always drawn to those so unwilling to share this kind of grace? I was desperate to find the answer to that question. I knew changes were imperative. I never wanted to be swept off my feet again. But, if I did, it would be by the Holy Spirit.

This time I would erect a wall around my heart, impenetrable to those *less than special* connections. There was even an iron gate around that wall and no one was getting in, not even if he showed up on a white horse, flags waving and covered in polished 24 karat gold. I was building a fortress. It was the only way I could protect myself.

If I could keep pain from getting through the walls of my heart, I would feel like I had some sense of control. As I would find out soon enough, no amount of control could ease the pain of being alone, and feeling so alone just made me angry.

It was difficult to admit that I was angry, but I was. Admitting it gave all the power to those who had hurt me. I knew my only choice was to let go of my anger, but that was easier said than done. It was okay to be angry, but now what to do with it.

"Be angry and sin not." ~ Ephesians 4:26

Placing blame wasn't an option, nor finding fault, so finding a solution became my mission. Focus on what I *could* control and that was a very short list. The enemy had a way of making me feel weak, wanting me to live scared and unprepared, but God was preparing me. If this was the dragon I was to slay, I was going to be ready for the battle. My hatred for living in fear was my motivation.

During moments on my knees I heard answers, but sometimes none came. Not a day went by without tears. I had accepted the cross that was now mine to carry, but the idea that the whole life I knew was gone was too much to bear alone. I wasn't prepared for that.

It changed not only my past and my present, but would definitely alter my *Happily Even After.* My wounds were too deep for mending. I felt completely broken, and some things just can't be unbroken. I was begging for someone to prove me wrong. His word said He could.

Pity Party

***"He heals the brokenhearted and binds up their wounds." ~
Psalm 147:3***

A little ice cream didn't hurt either. I remember on many occasions when ice cream stopped the flow of tears for a bit. Maybe it wasn't really the ice cream, but the sense of empathy I felt in its delivery. My friend Stephanie was always willing to share in it, and, it didn't seem to carry as much guilt when shared over a good cry.

I really wasn't one for pity, nevertheless, my *party of one* life was beginning whether I liked it or not. At least I had company. Steph was with me through it all. She listened and tried to understand. I teased her quite a bit about her bleeding ears. I just knew they must have been raw listening to my sob story over and over.

She was always ready and willing to comfort me. There were nights when her home became mine and the warmth of her friendship wrapped me with love and safety, but mostly I felt understood. I knew she was no stranger to loss.

Her husband was killed in a tragic car accident years before, leaving her alone with a 2 year old baby girl. She worked hard, raised a daughter and opened her home, not just to me but many others during times of need. I knew if anyone could relate, she could.

While I was there with her, warmth flowed. Just the sound of someone else breathing was life giving. I tried to sense the same warmth in those few months following my short stay there, as I ventured into my own empty house. It didn't welcome me the same, at least not at first.

It was smaller than I was accustomed to, but even still, I couldn't bring myself to move out of the bedroom. I would venture into my study occasionally, and only went to the kitchen to stand at the counter alone eating my meals quickly before returning to the safety of my blanket.

I felt as if a stranger were lurking outside my window planning his attack. He was waiting to sneak up on me, and it always made me uneasy. I hated hearing the faint whisper in my ear, reminding me I was alone, completely alone.

I felt helpless and needy. I didn't want to admit to anyone that I could feel so in need. I was strong but at times knew I was miles from it. Those are times reserved for true besties. The phone I held tightly clutched in my hand saved me at the moment it rang. Silence was deafening and a phone called was a welcomed distraction.

"I'm fine." I said before she could even ask, "or I will be." Stephanie had a way of knowing what I was saying when I wasn't saying anything at all. "I'm coming over. Which flavor ice-cream do you want, Cookies n Cream or Butter Pecan?" She asked.

"I don't want you to drive all the way over here to baby sit me." I said with prideful tears welling up. We lived 30 minutes away from each other now and I couldn't bear the idea of someone going so far out of their way for me.

"Okay then, I'm bringing both. I'll be there in a few." She responded abruptly. I knew I was destined to learn to receive love, even if I didn't feel worthy of it.

Steph felt the desperation in my voice, and knew what I needed. Like lightening, she came, chick flick in one hand, and two quarts of our favorite ice cream in the other. Her prescription included a full box of tissues, several different toppings and of course, Diet Coke to balance it all out. What else could I do, other than enjoy a night of chick flick therapy, and we started with a good one, *The Holiday*.

"...And after all that, however long all that may be, you'll go somewhere new. And you'll meet people who make you feel worthwhile again. And little pieces of your soul will finally come back." ~ The Holiday, movie

I found myself pondering that quote, as if I was trying to convince myself, this little morsel of wisdom might even be true for someone like me. It had to be true. I wasn't going anywhere new, but I would meet new people who would make me feel worthwhile again. I *needed* pieces of my soul to come back. I knew I couldn't have a *Happily Even After* without them.

We loved watching our favorites to remind ourselves the whole world could be upside down, and in just two short hours, right side up again. The ones that made our play list always ended, *Happily Even After.*

I lived vicariously through the actors on the screen, memorized quotes to make myself feel better, and recited them during the rough spots. They made me believe if it could work for them, it could work for me. Since life hadn't killed me, it was making me stronger. It would have killed me had I let it, and knowing life was fragile, made me all the more desperate to live it.

"Do you know the most surprising thing about divorce? It doesn't actually kill you. Like a bullet to the heart or a head-on car wreck, it should. When someone you've promised to cherish till death do you part says, "I never loved you," it should kill you instantly. You shouldn't have to wake up day after day after that, trying to understand how in the world you didn't know. The light just never went on, you know. I must have known, of course, but I was too scared to see the truth. Then fear just makes you so stupid." ~ Under The Tuscan Sun, movie

Well, I didn't want to be stupid, so I hung on for dear life, to my family, friends, church, work and I prayed like the dickens.

Friends were a great comfort to me. I knew emotional moments like this would come again with every sunrise and sunset. Some moments would be filled with gratitude, and others with desperation. Some days were filled with peace and comfort while others were full of anger and pain. God met me there each time.

He's not afraid, confused or surprised by my emotions because He fashioned me Himself. With His patience He wrapped His arms around me, engulfing every part of me. His perfect timing moved me just far enough out of my own self to get me through one more day.

Can You Hear Me God? ~

Disappointments, failures and emotional pain are corrosive and chip away at relationships like a cancer, making you feel unheard. Just because I *felt* unheard, didn't mean I was, and just because I couldn't hear God's voice, didn't mean He wasn't speaking. But was I listening? Maybe I just didn't want to hear His answer. Maybe I was crying out to God for what *I* wanted, without regard to what *He* wanted for me.

Since I was alone at this particular venture, it *must* have been His will. Still, I wanted my own way, and lost myself once again in the search for fairy tales. I wasn't sure if there was a degree in loosing yourself, but if there was, I was majoring in it. From childhood, as I turned things upside down, I expected God to make all things right side up again.

"If you never expect anything, you will never be disappointed."
~ Ben Franklin

Expectations had become my weakness. I had them, got hurt, cried, then got angry. My anger was not only with myself, but also with God. I needed Him to hear me, or maybe I just needed to hear myself say it. *I'm angry with You, God.* It didn't come as a shock to Him though. He knew where I was headed before I took my first step. I was being a bit rebellious and He had the answers I needed.

Like my granddaughter Rylee, who was spending the day with me. She was 7, and being a little more rebellious than I prefer. So, she was sentenced to time alone in her bedroom. Turning her rebellion around, and apologizing for her behavior was her penance. Only then could she be released from her dungeon.

If you've ever heard a 7 year-old little girl squeal like she had just gotten a new puppy, Rylee was two of those put together. I often wondered how her vocal chords survived the abuse. They must have been bleeding that day. She cried for a half hour or so. Begging took the form of screams, flooding the room as I sat calmly on the floor with her brother, Landon, enjoying some cuddle time.

Poking her little red nose out of the crack in the door, she demanded freedom. I remember thinking to myself *her stamina will be an asset one day.* She assumed I couldn't hear her, because she kept screaming louder as I continued to look the other way.

Of course I heard her!

By this time the whole neighborhood did too, loud and clear. I *was* listening, but waiting for her to calm down, quiet herself, and come humbly to receive the love I had been waiting to give all along. We would *all* be happy when she did, especially Landon, who was afraid to move an inch from the safety of my arms.

There wasn't one moment that I didn't hear her cries. There was never a time I wasn't listening. I chose not to respond until her heart was right. For a brief moment our fellowship was interrupted, but my love for her never wavered. I knew what was best for her that day and when she finally emerged, broken and humbled, she came sweetly and said those two words we all love and need to hear, *"I'm sorry."*

That was all I needed. All the love a Grandma has to give came flooding into the room, and our relationship was immediately restored.

> *God's loyal love couldn't have run out, his merciful love couldn't have dried up. They're created new every morning. How great your faithfulness! I'm sticking with God (I say it over and over). He's all I've got left. ~*
> *Lamentations 3: 22-24 Message Bible*

God's love is just like that. He's waiting to pour out His love on us if we will come humbly to Him and say those two words. He's not *all we have left.* **He's ALL WE HAVE.** His patience never runs out and His mercy is new every day, because He creates it again and again.

> *God proves to be good to the man who passionately waits to the woman who diligently seeks. It's a good thing to quietly hope, quietly hope for help from God. It's a good thing when you're young to stick it out through the hard times."*
> *Lamentations 3: 25-27 Message Bible*

God is here listening, hearing and knows when it's best not to respond. He is a loving Father and only wants the best for me. I may not understand or like the silence. I may not like waiting, trusting or being alone while I cry out in pain, but God *is* listening. He hears. He's compassionate, and good. I quietly hope, and quietly wait on Him. Even before I uttered my first word, He had already forgiven me.

"Therefore, there is now no condemnation for those who are in Christ." Romans 8:1

I was *in* Christ. I knew that for sure. He never condemned me, and He proved himself to be faithful. So, what did I have to fear?

~ *"Strong women don't play victim, don't make themselves look pitiful, and don't point fingers. They stand and deal."* ~

Mandy Hale

Chapter Eight

~ *Have No Fear* ~

Why was I so scared when I appeared to be a strong woman otherwise? I couldn't for the life of me figure out how to walk through this life, even with the hope I found in Christ, without fear.

He who fears the Lord is never alarmed, never afraid; for the Lord is his hope. ~Sirach 34:14 New American Bible

People say it's good to have a *healthy* fear. Is there such a thing as *healthy* fear? All I know is it didn't seem good for my health at all. Everything I was experiencing gave wings to that dragon. It had to be vanquished and for good, if it was even possible. Maybe I needed to grip tightly the fear that was gripping me, and around its throat might be best. It only seemed fair.

I didn't want to hand over the keys to my heart so easily ever again. To place my heart in someone else's care equaled pain in my book. I had been let down so much in the past, and women I loved had been too. Every Prince Charming carried so much baggage of their own: past hurts, past loves.

I started to wonder if any man came without the faint scent of another woman's perfume? Their fragrance, along with their desires, lingered around my Prince Charming. They certainly wore out their welcome with me. It seemed I had the same battle with every man whom I shared my journey. It was up to me to slay that dragon, win that war and make that man forget she ever existed. Was that just a fairy tale too? Even for the best of us, that would take a miracle.

It all sounded a little cliché, but I found myself thanking God for those *unanswered prayers*. Hardening my resolve was a better option than hardening my heart, but I could sense the tenderness waning as time marched on. Since protecting itself from further pain was now my heart's primary objective. Giving up seemed the best option. It was the way of least resistance. I thought love wasn't supposed to hurt, but it was causing *me* pain.

I was traveling down a whole different path now and confusion was becoming a way of life. Without the slightest hesitation I opened doors that should have remained closed, and climbed through windows I had no business even cracking. All in hopes of finding true love. If it wanted to be found, it wasn't making things easy for me.

I was so focused on doors and windows that I was missing what lay right under my feet, the road I traveled. It could take me anywhere I wanted to go. I had to choose to keep moving forward. Maybe I would simply step into my own *Happily Even After.* If only I wasn't so afraid.

I had come to the realization that I feared rejection, pain, hurt, change, challenge, commitment, you name it, I was afraid of it. I spent the better part of my life, out of fear, hiding behind ministry, family, friends and yes, my wedding ring. I had erected walls all around me. It was where I found safety and protection.

I made excuses for not trying new things or reaching higher. But I remembered a quote from a very wise woman, Joyce Meyer. *"Just because you feel fear doesn't mean you can't do something, just do it afraid."* I could never let fear stop me ever again. I was the daughter of a king, *the* King to be exact, and that made me a princess. He promised.

"Nothing will I withhold from those who walk uprightly." Psalm 84:11

It came with provision, protection and all the unbroken promises a girl could dream of. So why was I still afraid? Why did I still feel so empty?

Webster's Dictionary says empty means to be *"abandoned"*. I certainly felt that way. But it also means to be *"ineffective, useless, void, meaningless, hollow or insubstantial"*. I was certain I was none of those things. Jesus Himself made me effective, useful and definitely substantial.

I had to find it within myself. I was single, and lonely at times, but not empty. If there was any emptiness in me, it was longing to be filled by the Holy Spirit. God promised never to leave me nor forsake me.

Be strong and courageous. Do not fear or be in dread of them, for it is the LORD your God who goes with you. He will not leave you or forsake you." Deuteronomy 31:6

I knew I wasn't alone, but would I ever feel worthy of a Prince? The enemy didn't want me to think so. He wanted me to believe I wasn't good enough. He wanted me to believe I was unwanted, and I started to believe him. I told myself the lies weren't true, but I actually started to live life as though they were. I lived "sick", as my girlfriend Mandy called it while describing her own personal journey with illness.

"It's when you carry sadness within yourself," She said. I was hiding behind happy eyes, forced smiles and a false, anxious laughter. I needed to stop living sick. She said, "Claim healing in Jesus' name, send the enemy scrambling for a new tactic and start living unafraid. God's got this, and you!" She exclaimed.

Then why did I put up walls? Why did I want so desperately to be held and comforted yet avoid it for fear that someone might come along and do just that? Maybe I believed he wouldn't truly mean it? Maybe he'd see how vulnerable I was. Maybe I was just a burden anyway.

There's nothing in the world wrong with wanting to be loved and comforted by another human being. I had to be willing to ask for it and surround myself with those who were willing to give it. True love conquers all fear.

Have No Fear

"There is no fear in love. But perfect love drives out fear, because fear has to do with punishment. The one who fears is not made perfect in love." 1 John 4:18 NIV

Fear seemed to surround me. I had choices to make about my future that I wasn't ready to make and first needed time to figure out who I truly was. These choices would be life altering, and could affect those I cared about, but walking around on eggs shells was not a choice I wanted to make. The possibility of affecting those lives negatively made me feel completely paralyzed.

I was certain that one wrong move would set me on a course to disaster. I was becoming a pro at wrong moves. I wanted to follow Christ. I wanted to be in His will for sure, but how was I supposed to know which way that meant. Was there one path or many? Which one was I supposed to be on? I couldn't make sense of it and wanted God to spell it out in the clouds.

I begged God to speak clearly. "God, I'm serving you. I'm following you. I have given my life to you, everything I am." I said. Like Frances, in *Under The Tuscan Sun*, pleading her case with the Blessed Virgin Mary. *"What more can I do?"* I cried. I had already done, and then done more, I thought.

I just wasn't sure I had enough courage to do anything else at all, especially if I couldn't trust. Trust is, to me, the absolute foundation for any relationship, confidant or spouse. Lack of it repels relationships, and disappoints the people around us, causing great divides.

Successful relationships are built on a foundation of mutual respect and trust. If I could no longer trust anyone, not even myself, my only option appeared to be loneliness. I already felt so alone. I hid my heart away behind the wall I had erected. I could choose never to trust or love again, or I could continue to believe my *Happily Even After* was still out there for me to discover.

What was God teaching me for the next chapter? How could I make my dream come true? The real question I asked myself was, *"Is joy found only when a dream is realized, or is it found in the journey to attain it?"* I wasn't going to find out by sitting around waiting for it to fall in my lap.

I knew if I was still here, God wasn't finished with me. He had a plan for me, but healing would have to take place first. You just can't miss that step.

Time heals, so I'm told. I was hopeful at first, but an eviction was taking place in my heart. Sad and fearful emotions were driving away happy and hopeful ones. There wasn't much room in my heart for anything more than crushed dreams. It was deeply and physically painful.

Everyone at some point in their life has either said or heard the words, "Time heals all wounds". They say, "In time things will work out." Who were *they* anyway and how did they know so much about time? I truly believed that no amount of time was gonna heal my wounds because it caused me to question every kindness shown me.

Have you ever noticed how those four words slip off of your tongue like melted butter on a piping hot biscuit when you offer them to a friend? Well, there's nothing ooey gooey about those four little words when you're on the receiving end, no melted butter anywhere, only dry crusty bread. Time doesn't heal anything, God does.

It's easy to remind people that with time, they'll get better, but it's also easier said than done. I told myself it would get easier with time, memories would fade and distractions would take their place. But I can remember exactly how, where and when I got each scar, so they aren't likely forgotten.

No one knows what to say or do for you when you're hurting, as if we're actually supposed to do anything at all. I think we feel as if it isn't okay to feel pain so we cover it up with a very thin Band-Aid, hoping not to bring too much attention to our pain.

I didn't want sympathy. That meant people would feel sorry for me, but may or may not be moved to do anything at all about it. Empathy. Now that was a different story. That meant someone would sit down with me, share my pain and let me hurt or cry, experiencing every gut wrenching feeling.

True empathy cries with the broken hearted and when all the tears lie in a puddle on the ground, you can't tell one from another. That's when the healing begins. It doesn't try to fix things, but realizes that it may actually be in the *not fixing* that we take the first steps in doing so. Everyone needs a friend like that, who sticks closer than a brother, God.

"A man of many companions may come to ruin, but there is a friend who sticks closer than a brother." ~Proverbs 18:24 ESV

I surrounded myself with people who loved me, and truly had empathy for me. They were the reason I was still kicking in the first place, reminding me light was at the end of this tunnel, even if I couldn't see it yet. I was truly blessed.

I would heal in God's time and the puddle on the ground would dry up eventually. I knew many other couples, like my aunt and uncle, who experienced great pain, but without it, they would not have found each other. It would be the same for me if I could be patient and trust God.

Some of my wounds were so deep, they required mending from the inside out and only God can do that. These wounds take the longest to heal, need the most care and leave the biggest scars and that's the kind I had. With His healing and His timing, I'd become stronger. God intended for me to persevere through my pain. He didn't want me to get lost in a puddle on the ground, but to see my reflection there and in it, His likeness.

Healing included getting over the past, letting go of the guilt, changing directions, and moving full steam ahead. It was like peddling a bike straight ahead as fast as my feet could move. If I just moved forward, I would eventually arrive at a place I longed for, but all I ever arrived at was exhaustion.

Somewhere in a rush of wind, I heard that still small voice say; *just keep peddling. Change gears, hold onto the handlebars and turn the corner.* As I did, the view immediately changed. This street was lined with spectators. Like I was leading a parade. They were strangers yet they rooted for me just the same. Clouds once covering the sky moved away to let the sun peek through.

My healing was never down that dusty road I was first traveling, though I had spent much of my energy peddling there. It wasn't until I changed gears and turned the corner I found it. The message seemed clear. One street was lonely and led to disappointment, the other full of hope and others to share the burden. I couldn't do it alone.

God put people in my life to help my wounds heal completely. Unfortunately, my fear usually pushed them away. God knows exactly what He's doing. There are no chance meetings. They are only divine appointments. I had seen many of these appointments.

Some couples had been together now for a lifetime, but I knew there were others who had been given a second chance at *Happily Even After*, like my aunt and uncle Oh the love they would have missed, had fear kept my Aunt Joan in a prison cell.

She was madly in love with my Uncle John, and he was no less in love with her. I will never forget the way he called her sweetie pie as she sat in his bear-like lap. He certainly had a twinkle in his eye for her and withheld nothing if he thought it would make her happy.

He was a rather large man, the most kind, soft spoken and gentle teddy bear to ever love this princess. Their "*once upon a time*" was far from perfect but they both found healing in their *Happily Even After*.

Aunt Joan created quite a few puddles herself over the years and desperately wanted a second chance. She and Uncle John found a fairy tale within their two messed up lives. It's a good thing he didn't take her advice to *drive on down the road* because her life was changed forever, even with a fresh batch of struggle.

It's funny how life can change on a dime. One minute I was on top of the world and the next minute I felt six feet under. This life was certainly not the one I had chosen for myself. God only knows how long it will take for the clouds to clear and the light to shine through.

If life repeats itself, I was sure to be in and out of the clouds over and over again until my last breath. Thank God there was someone in the clouds with me. His name is Jesus. One thing for sure, He had surrounded me with love.

"Too many of us are not living our dreams because we are too busy living our fears." ~ *Les Brown*

Chapter Nine

~ *Drive On Down The Road* ~

It didn't start out like a fairy tale, but true love and real life would begin to reveal one as the years unveiled a beautiful love story of which only a few can boast. Aunt Joan sat at my kitchen table sipping hot tea and sharing her heart with me. It was precious.

This story begins with the death of a very tumultuous marriage to her first husband and father of her three children. Their love affair would fade quickly as abuse reared its ugly head. Aunt Joan was looking for a bright light in a very dark place, and at the end of a very short rope. She found herself fresh out of divorce court with three children. Without the ability to support them, life hung by a thread and fear was her only friend.

Her ex-husband, taking advantage of her weakness, whisked the children away to start over, without the mother who had given them life. Aunt Joan was devastated. "He said the only way he would support me was if I let him have the children", she recalled. "He said we would share the responsibilities. I felt I had no other option, so I agreed."

She let them go. However, the plan abruptly changed with his decision to hide them in New York, far out of her reach. When she tried to find them, she was met with indifference. He had, in her words, "indoctrinated" them. "He taught them to call me by my first name." she said sadly. " There is nothing that could break a mother's heart more than that."

She tried to arrange for sharing the children but he threatened her life if she attempted to do so. There was nowhere to turn, so she complied. He took the kids and left with no intentions of being in touch with her ever again.

Aunt Joan wasn't looking for anything at this point except perhaps a job. Friends came to her rescue, offering her a job as a waitress at a nearby tavern, so she made a plan to start her life over. Now the last thing she wanted was to meet Prince Charming in an old tavern, but whether or not she wanted to find one there, find him she did.

His name was John. They called him Big John, because he was just that. "Wow, you sure are cute." He said as He put his hand on her waist. "Please take your hands off of me you goon." She responded. "If I want you to touch me, I'll let you know."

With that, He replied, "Oooh, she's got spunk." He liked girls with spunk and spice and she had no shortage of either. She quickly let him know she wouldn't touch him with a ten-foot pole. Aunt Joan had rules, and liking a guy more than he liked her was not one of them. She was on a mission to show him that she was going to keep it that way. He didn't seem to mind, because he liked the chase.

"He had this great big smile on his face and said okay." She explained. It never did stop his advances, though. He seemed to crave more. He came in again, and offered to buy her a beer. "I said, no thanks, I don't drink beer." She barked back. He asked again, as if he thought she might have changed her mind in the last two seconds. "No, no and no! What about NO do you not understand?" She questioned.

If Uncle John was nothing else, he was persistent. She was interested in someone else by this time, or so she thought. She couldn't help but find herself strangely drawn to a man she refused to pay any attention to. This was certainly a divine appointment.

My uncle's luck changed when she became a "blubbering inebriated mess" in her words. She returned to the tavern to take John up on the beer he had promised and for one who said she didn't drink, she surely made a liar out of herself that night. The one she was blubbering all of this heartache to was, none other than, John Stokes, the 'goon', who minutes before was not worthy of a ten-foot pole. When her friends discovered she had one too many beers, they asked John to take her home.

Since driving was out of the question at that point, Uncle John took her to get a cup of coffee and a sandwich. "Just what I wanted after being slightly drunk." Aunt Joan mumbled under her breath.

He was a perfect gentleman, ordering a coffee and grilled cheese sandwich. She drank the coffee but he ate the sandwich and then took her to her apt. He sat her down on the couch and asked her if she needed him to stay. "No." She said sternly. "I told you I wouldn't touch you with a ten-foot pole." So Uncle John went home.

His diligence paid off and just eight months later they were married. Of course there were a few things to accomplish before the nuptials, like meeting the new mother-in-law. It was just a small hill to climb for the introduction of one feisty young, slightly rebellious girl and one-well, you'll see.

Uncle John's mom was a born again, blood bought, God fearing, bible believing, Church of God lady. Though she wasn't the judgmental type, she greeted Aunt Joan with a big hug and said, "Sit down honey. I think we may need to talk." Aunt Joan was wearing a pair of slim tight pants, a midriff top and had a cigarette hanging out of her mouth. Though their two lives were vastly different, it wasn't long at all before they became great friends.

"Her influence was incredible in my life." Aunt Joan said. "She never judged me, scolded me or ever told me my pants were to tight or that I shouldn't be smoking cigarettes. She just loved me with the love of Jesus, and what an example she was in my life."

Aunt Joan and Uncle John were married on December 19, 1964 and they joined John's mom for Christmas shortly after. "How do you like my new wife?" He asked. The response was the beginning of a life changing time for Joan, as she heard her new mother in law reply, "I love her to pieces." Through the example of Uncle John's Mom, my Aunt Joan found her way back to the Lord.

Often when he didn't join her for church, she went anyway. He was only interested in some male bonding over a few beers with his buddies, but Joan sternly warned him if this was his choice, they would be over. "We are going to live for the Lord or we will not be together at all." She demanded. As any Prince charming would do, he changed his lifestyle and just about everything else from that moment on.

Four years later God answered their prayers with the birth of Sherry Anne, their only child. She had no contact with her other children, and since John had no other children, Sherry became the whole focus of their fairy tale life together.

By this time Uncle John had a great sales position with the Pepsi Cola Company and clearly loved his job. He won vacations in the United States, England and Scotland. They visited the Bahamas, St Thomas, San Francisco, and the Grand Canyon. "It was great to be able to get away on mini vacations", she said. Although, there was one drawback for Aunt Joan, she was grateful for the job, and the money it provided, but she got tired of all the high society parties they were required to attend.

After staying with Pepsi for many years, she thought he might be willing to walk away, take her somewhere, buy a business and live Happily Ever after. She wasn't sure, just hoping, but her Prince Charming couldn't say no to his princess, so he did just that, but the *Happily Ever After* never came.

They had bought a small truck stop in Al. and after three years, their daughter was so unhappy she threatened to run away. They even bought her a horse of her very own, hoping to make things better, but she was still very unhappy.

Aunt Joan felt as if the horse was just an escape vehicle of the four-legged kind for Sherry. They knew it wasn't working when they found her crying day after day. She prayed that God would change things and He did.

Someone came to buy the truck stop, so they packed everything and back to Florida they went. They prayed about what to do and it only seemed appropriate that he go back to work for Pepsi right away.

Now they were back to a more normal life in Tampa at a familiar place and familiar job. Little did they know their daughter would require their undivided focus, and attention. Life would once again take some major twists and turns. It would either make or break their marriage.

My aunt and uncle were never more tested and tried, but it would prove to be a bonding agent that sealed their relationship to the very last day. They dealt together with their daughter on everything from School, a three-year detour in California, Chicken Pox, Anorexia and Bulimia, career decisions and dating choices. They walked their daughter through every stage hand in hand only more solidifying their commitment to each other and to their family.

It robbed them of almost 6 years of their life, but God finally gave Sherry freedom from the disease. They were hoping that a lasting love would come into her life, but Sherry didn't buy into fairy tales, so after being accepted into veterinary school in Grenada, West Indies, she started a new life for herself.

They were finally able now to focus on one another. However, this was a huge valley in their relationship. "John was as supportive as a wet paper plate." Aunt Joan remembers. This season would require her to trust God more than she had ever trusted Him before. Not only was her daughter moving miles away, but also Uncle John was restructured out of his job at Pepsi after 30 years.

God definitely had his hand on their lives. After healing their daughter's anorexia, they learned to trust in Him alone. Although Aunt Joan said she wouldn't touch him with a ten-foot pole, Uncle John's love for her drew them closer than she could've ever imagined.

He didn't put on errs or sway in his beliefs, and was never a phony. "Try to find one of those today, it aint easy." Aunt Joan said. "I haven't found anyone like him since. I know they are out there but how do you find one?" Aunt Joan's motto said: *If he aint a*

Christian, just drive on down the road. If they aren't willing to put you above everything else, except God, don't bother. Drive on by.

God said to "love your wife as Christ loves the church". If he isn't willing to love you like that, you're best to just stick with God alone. I believe many women make that mistake today. They don't plan for the long haul. They want it now and they'll just trade up if things don't work out.

"All I have to say is make sure he loves Jesus first. If he does, then he'll put you first. If he doesn't, then drive on down the road." Aunt Joan finished. " It has been thirteen years since John's passing, but I still miss him so much. After God, he was my rock. I doubt I would ever find that kind of love, ever again, and at 77 years old, I 'aint really looking but I still believe in Love," she concluded with confidence.

It's hard to believe that people really do love each other even beyond the end of their Happily Even After story. I guess life goes on, love goes on and it's re-birthed into a whole new and beautiful story as we retell it to those who love the real life and real love of two hearts that were bound together by struggle, and trust.

"The man who can drive himself further once the effort gets painful, is the man who will win." ~
Roger Bannister

Chapter Ten

~ *Sweet Dreams* ~

I hoped one day to have the kind of relationship my aunt and uncle had. I could at least dream about it. The hope of sweet dreams gave me reason to close my eyes each night. It was a way to escape. My pillow was one friend who knew every secret. Counting every tear, it knew me well.

If I was going to find a fairy tale, maybe one night I might find it there. It seemed to be the only place fairy tales really existed, in my dreams. What did my dreamland look like?

As a child full of hope, it was a fairy tale land. As a young adult, it was a place where you could smell grandma's apple pie cooling in the window. The sounds of a well-hit baseball mixed with some vivid color commentary came from the living room leaving no doubt you were experiencing history in the making. Iced tea was steeping on the kitchen table, eagerly awaiting an overabundance of sugar that never seemed to cause us any harm.

Family members gathered in anticipation of what was always a finger licking good time. Hugs and smiles were in great supply, and the young ones gathered around as their elders sang songs and spoke of the good ole days.

When we found our partner, we walked through life hand in hand and our hearts connected and purposed to fulfill a calling on our lives with someone we had chosen to walk it out with. We were encouraged to make it work at all cost and expected to do no less.

We weren't given options to the contrary, nor did we desire any. We held fast to the notion that if all was well with us, all was well with the world. Was that just a dream, the good old days that were now gone forever?

My reality was being my only companion in life, with a whole lot more alone time than I ever imagined. If I was going to be true to myself, then everyone would discover the real woman behind the fake smiles, the real person I had abandoned years ago.

I wasn't sure if that was a good thing or not. The essence of who I truly was would come to the surface, good or bad. I literally conversed with no one other than myself, and God, and the deepest parts of my inner being were revealed.

I dreamed for that one special moment, when time stands still and my heart finally found its match and felt whole for the first time. I didn't really *need* a man to feel whole. God alone could do that. But this void in my heart was created to draw me together with that one special connection He designed Himself.

Like Snow White, I found myself *wishing for the one I love to find me*. As if I was lost. I'm not sure what I was really wishing for. I wasn't hiding but I wasn't necessarily trying to be found either. I was too afraid to move forward, but even more afraid not to.

I knew deep down that I might be in search of someone who existed only in my dreams. Was I expecting too much? Even a great man couldn't be my God. I didn't need a god. I didn't particularly need a prince. I never saw myself as a princess anyway.

I was told that one day, someone would come along that would be worth the risk. Well this *dreamboat* better love like I did. That would be no simple task since I loved so hard. After God, I was praying he would at the very least love me as much as I loved him, not necessarily more, but certainly not less.

I wanted to be loved at my worst, knowing that I needed it most when I felt it least. I would never need to ask for space because it was given. I never wanted him to leave me alone, even though I might say I did. He would let me love him even when his strong armor refused to let me in, sensing that my love could melt his exterior without removing the strength that defined him.

I didn't want to be fixed and no matter how hard it seemed I might try, I neither wanted to, nor could I, fix him. If we lived close to God, with hope and our commitment to each other, the chord of three would be tested at times, but would never break. Could this really exist? It was my hope.

What would this dream guy possess that others didn't? If there was some sort of list of requirements and my imposed perfection encompassed most of them, it wouldn't take long for this damsel to figure out that *he* was not coming. I didn't stop believing in the *Happily Even After*, but I had to throw my list of requirements away. Maybe I should continue to wait it out, begging the universe to be mistaken, or throw caution to the wind and fall recklessly into anything resembling a fairy tale. Sadly I knew I would be left wanting.

Prince Charming was a figment of someone's very creative imagination. He, not only didn't possess this perfection I was told to look for, but he didn't exist at all. Neither did the Cinderella he had been searching for. There were moments I could see light flickering at the end of the tunnel but at times darkness overtook it.

If he *did* exist, would he be able to scale the wall made of stone I built around my heart? Was I even giving him a reason to? What was behind that wall? Would he find a heart as hard as the stone guarding it? Or was the wall protecting a softened heart that could still be broken? Was it protecting a strong and confident heart, one that welcomed his gallant efforts?

Maybe the suit my Prince wore would be fashioned by the armor protecting my heart. The only way he could do that was for me to give it to him. I just hoped, as my prince reached out and took my heart in his hands, he would see *Handle With Care* written all over it, and I prayed he knew how to read.

My heart was fragile but it was healing. The scars making my heart stronger were reminders that, though it was capable of being broken, it was also capable of being mended. God was my healer and I knew my heart would soften in time. I had no choice but to trust God and I wasn't looking for another option.

The designer of the Universe, the one who handcrafted me, knows the exact shape of my *empty* and certainly knows how to fill it. I wanted to believe He would. It's His timing that I didn't trust. If I was being honest with myself, I was completely impatient with God. I had no choice but to wait it out. In the meantime, I was required to make peace with my *empty*.

I either trusted God, or I didn't. I wanted to trust Him, but once I turned over the controls, I'd snatch them back before I could see progress. I just couldn't be still and rest in the promise that God has my life in His hands. He wants me to live an abundant life. He'll provide all I need if I'll let go. Even if it wasn't when, or how, I expected.

I didn't realize that Prince Charming might show up without the white horse, and with his shining armor a little more smudged than I expected, not like my dreams. If he was worth the risk, he might even be unrecognizable. I was at a place in my life when I didn't expect him to show up at all.

In my dreams, Prince Charming would sweep me off my feet and take me off to the land of milk and honey where there was no sadness, pain or heartache. It was a beautiful and happy place I wanted to stay forever. I'd watch the sun melt away on the horizon and in the quiet and calm, hear it sigh as it bid farewell to its audience. Sadly, that place doesn't exist.

Life is too full of *real*. I had been lulled to sleep. The line between real and fairy tale was being blurred daily. Even reality TV didn't contain all that much real. Apparently I had to wake up to my *own* reality this time and falling for the next Prince Charming was *one* way to do it. I always chose the long and hard way around any lesson.

When God created Adam and said it wasn't good for him to be alone, He didn't create for him a job, kids, friends or hobbies. He created the *one thing* that He knew Adam couldn't do without. The *one thing* that could make Adam complete, a perfect complement, a partner.

God knew if man choose wisely, he would have a woman by his side giving wings to his vision, and not hinder him in his walk towards the future he sought for himself and those he cared for. Woe to the man who chooses poorly.

"A continual dripping on a rainy day and a quarrelsome wife are alike." ~ Proverbs 27:15 ESV

I recently attended a marriage conference my friend, Dr. Richard Marks taught. He said, God really did intend for Adam to be united with Eve. If communion with God was all he needed to be whole, Adam had that.

What he lacked was his female counterpart to commune and connect intimately with. There is no other relationship like the one God intended. He fashioned the union of two separate beings, male and female, to represent His love for us, and to accomplish great things in the Earth.

Unconditional love and sacrifice for each other should be our gift back to Him. He designed someone to challenge me, love me, protect me, encourage me, and even sharpen the dull edges at times. Together, we should be full of love and full of the grace it takes to see each other's flaws vulnerably exposed and still find 'us' incredibly satisfying. God wrapped us as one perfectly designed gift for each other. There is nothing else in creation that fits together quite like we do. We're not perfect, but God's design is.

Did Mr. Worth the risk exist? There was a small part of me that desperately longed for it to be true. I didn't want to settle for Mr. *Right Now.* I kept a flame burning for him inside the walls of my heart. It was like lighting a candle for a missing loved one.

My Prince Charming was missing. I knew now, when I found him, he might not be riding a white horse or wearing any armor at all. Instead of waving flags, he would need a sledgehammer to knock down these walls. I was praying that my *Mr. Worth The Risk* was carrying one.

I found out, I wasn't gonna be rescued by anything or anyone but God Himself, The One who came to rescue me once and for all. I had to lay *self* down in order to be rescued, just as I would have to give my heart to my rescuer. I had to walk away from *me* and walk towards Him. I would have to wait for Prince Charming, but I hoped he *would* be worth it.

God will send you the right man at the right time, I was told many times. I knew this concept. I had said it to others on occasion. I was stubborn, though. How ridiculous it was to jump in again so quickly after such a painful year, but jump I did, with Prince Charming # 3. I was sure I'd find true love, this time. What did I have to lose, but a few more pieces of my heart?

~ "A dream is a wish your heart makes." ~

Unknown

Chapter Eleven

~ *Land Of Unicorns And Rainbows* ~

When I was young, I believed in, *all you need is love.* As I began to mature, I realized it takes a whole lot more than that. I had come to the ripe old age of *it takes everything* to experience that kind of love, commitment and loyalty, selflessly giving, loving, forgiving and praying daily. It takes every part of "US" to make it Happily Even After.

I was beginning to feel a bit overwhelmed. "I don't want to be alone." I cried. I didn't want to feel alone, even if I was alone. I didn't feel safe. Safety came in the form of a wedding ring, and I had worn my safety for the last 31 years. I was sure I was ready to love again even without the false protection a ring would give. Moving forward was my only hope.

I wasn't going to give up on love just because it gave up on me, even if it had proven itself to be a bit unfair. I was taught not to give up so easily and I believed what I was searching for was out there waiting to be found. If I *truly* didn't want to feel alone, I had no other option.

Although, God had already promised me He'd never leave me, I managed to continue moving along the same path, with even more determination. At every detour there was new possibility, and this time was no exception. I looked up and he was there, searching for the same thing.

He was waiting there for me in a lavender shirt, shorts and sandals, and wearing an irresistible smile. Kindness was in his eyes and his voice could calm the roughest seas. It seemed a few of our friends had plans about where the two of us might fit in each other's fairy tale. So he opened up the possibilities, and began our two and a half hour conversation completely unaware of where his words would take me.

"Just tell me to get lost." He said. "Tell me I'm out of my mind and I will go away and never bother you again."

I was intrigued by this shyness I had not seen before. We had a great conversation that night and agreed to pursue God and let Him work on the details. If it was meant to be, then taking it slow would be key in building this relationship, especially after having both been through divorce. Neither of us wanted to walk that road ever again.

We enjoyed our time together and said our goodbyes. I drove away that night not really sure of my next move, other than to pray about what God would have me do. There was a little spring in my step and an excitement in my heart that I welcomed. I had hope once again and I prayed all the way home that it was real.

"Trust Me", the Holy Spirit almost audibly said. "This is the path I have chosen for you. It is a sure path. It will be unfamiliar and unlike any other you have ever experienced. Don't over think it. Don't analyze it. Go with faith. I will not fail you, even when you don't understand. I know what's best for you and I am the only one who can deliver on that promise." It was hard to receive, but I believed He brought this man to me with a purpose.

So, the walls around my heart came tumbling down, not only because Mr. Charming was charming, not only because he said all the things I might have needed to hear, but literally because I wanted to give God a chance to prove Himself. If He did, I would have a front row seat to a miracle.

I quickly let Prince Charming go to town on the walls I had built, and the gate flung wide open. My heart rushed out onto my sleeve ready and waiting to be loved and appreciated like never before. I was never more full of hope and anticipation for what might lie ahead for me. *Could this be my Happily Even After?* I asked myself.

I woke each day to a reminder that I was loved and wanted. That was surely un-familiar. I looked forward to the hope of feeling safe once again. He made me believe I was worth loving, and I felt like a princess, for a whole month and a half.

Seems silly to me now, but I was in the land where fairy tales are born. It was *The Land of Unicorns and Rainbows.* This was a place where two people could sit for hours gazing into each other's eyes. Everything seemed perfect. Was I in a dream? I had to snap out of it, and I certainly would.

The flame burning inside my heart grew and I ran with it. But, there were storm clouds brewing on the horizon, and the fresh smell of rain was in the air. Our relationship burned out quicker than a match in a rainstorm. And, so went my fairy tale.

If I could just get my foot into that glass slipper, I thought. I felt a little like a *fool rushing in.* I simply had no choice but to back up, and let God pen my story Himself. He needed to author the next chapter of my life whether or not I let go of the pen.

When God took over the authoring of my story, it began to take on a more realistic appearance. Though I was seeing things more clearly, what seemed to be my *Happily Even After* was fading like the flame in my heart. Although I didn't want to admit it, nor did I want to accept it, the flame was being snuffed out. I wanted answers, but none were coming and my heart was broken once again.

No matter how carefully or how slowly someone breaks your heart, it's no less broken, and no matter what form it takes, rejection is still painful. Was this a test? Why was the instructor silent? Trust had been the underlying theme of this whole adventure, but I never imagined I would be tested this much. I was overwhelmed, motionless, speechless, and now, answerless.

Learning to let go was becoming a way of life. With each passing day there were reminders that I was holding on. Why was letting go so difficult? What did I have to gain from holding on so tightly?

How many of these lessons was I going to have to learn before realizing that waiting on Prince Charming was gonna take more of me than I wanted to give? All the wrong relationships came so quickly and easily. I suppose now that's why they never worked out.

"What happened to the path, God?" I begged. "Did You change Your mind? I thought You had chosen this path specifically for Me. What have I done wrong, and when will my heart stop hurting?"

With every question, one more wall went back up. It took me a while to figure it out, but I'm guessing now the path was just that, the path. Mr. Charming was not. He just happened to be on it, and for that short season brought with him something for me to learn, "Just do today", he reminded me over and over. God had, in His infinite wisdom, lined this path with a lesson I truly needed and could have learned in no other way.

We have a tendency to think that if it looks good and feels good it *must* be from God. That's not always the case. I found myself asking, "God, why do you dangle these carrots in front of me if they aren't for me?" Like every time before, the Holy Spirit spoke to me so clearly saying, *that wasn't me, and those aren't my carrots.*

Sometimes things that seem right may *not* be at all, not even close. I wanted the empty space filled. The enemy knows what I desire. He can dress it up in shining armor, sit it on a white horse and parade it in front of me all day long, but that doesn't mean it's what I need. So that's when I decided, I didn't like carrots anyway.

This time I wanted to live with my eyes wide open. I made a promise to myself that I would never fall in love again. I made a promise to God that I would never let a man take His place, and never lose myself in the Land of Unicorns and Rainbows.

I wasn't even capable of keeping that promise in the past, but moving forward, there were few options. Because I loved hard, I fell hard. It was as painful as any fall I had taken before and I was determined, if it was up to me, I would never feel that pain again.

That little chair in that little corner became a whole lot more real to me that day. The song I had sung as a little girl, from Cinderella, was exactly where I found myself. In the corner of my living room, in my very own chair, I sat night after night with my journal and, a box of tissue, wondering what I had done to get here, and what I was going to do to get out. I didn't realize I really didn't need an escape route. The path involved a little alone time. I just didn't receive the news so well.

Then I started singing that familiar song to myself. It went something like this.... *"In my own little corner, in my own little chair, I can be whatever I want to be."* When I think of the simple lyrics of Cinderella's song, I wonder why the message of her story eluded me. It didn't take long for the words to resonate with me this time. Could I really be whatever I chose to be? It was up to me, and only me. No one else could do it for me.

Unlike Cinderella, I just sat there weeping. She wasn't wondering why her Prince Charming hadn't come to rescue her or why he never climbed the walls of her castle that night. He didn't break down any doors, nor grab her up to carry her off to the ball that night. With determination, and a little help from a Fairy God Mother and a few friends, she got up, went by herself, and made a choice that night that changed her life forever.

Cinderella wasn't looking for a prince, she just wanted a dress and a new pair of shoes. So, I had to ask myself, why had I made my prince the music to which I danced? Why had I allowed the rhythm of his heart to conduct the beat of mine? It was no secret I had lost myself. I could now only vaguely remember the girl that use to look back at me in the mirror, for the fairy dust clouding my view.

I fell back into that small little corner and that small little chair mumbling the words to that song once again, "I can be whatever I want to be." Now I just had to figure out what "to be" looked like.

God put people in my life for me to love, but I wanted to be loved back. He said he loved me, but it wasn't enough. Circumstances made it impossible, but it didn't change God's plan. The path I was on was exactly where I was supposed to be.

I set out to put one foot in front of the other, *just doing today*, with a growing faith in God. My life verse had been the same since childhood.

"Trust the Lord with all your heart and lean not onto your own understanding; in all thy ways acknowledge Him and He shall direct thy paths." Proverbs 3:5 & 6 KJV

I was acknowledging God and I wanted to trust Him with all my heart. So with that in mind, I moved out of the *Land of Unicorns and Rainbows* to a land filled with potholes and detours. This land was certainly familiar, and I wasn't alone here.

My sister had been here before as well. She had experienced loss, rejection and failure. I remember days watching her plead her case with God, on the floor in a puddle of tears. It was painful and I knew that God was allowing me to empathize with her for the first time.

This wasn't the first time she had visited the land of potholes and would likely visit it again and again. But, she was here with me now. I was glad to have her compassion and help as I navigated through. I accepted my challenges here. There was much to gain if I stayed the course.

God never promised the path would be without potholes, but He promised to guide me through it. That proved, however painful, to be worth it as I grew stronger, learning to love with my will and not my feelings. It is the only way to spend an eternity with the one you truly love and I know God will be faithful to walk each step with me as I seek to find my Prince Charming, if he's out there.

"Everyone wants happiness. No one wants pain. But, you can't have a rainbow without a little rain." ~ Unknown

Chapter Twelve

~ *Runaway Bride* ~

My church had become my extended family, my people. Though exquisite, the building itself did little for me, but those who filled it did amazing things. Encouragement came in many forms, from the lyrics to my favorite songs, friends who became family, to the messages that came from the great men of the *Black Wood.*

"Know who you are and to whom you belong. Be passionate about it. There will be a struggle. You will go through the fire at times, and He'll be in there with you." Pastor Russ preached. He always pierced my soul with his clear and pragmatic words. As the service ended, He closed in prayer with a challenge and high hopes.

Most Sundays I would file out of the auditorium ready to conquer the world. Lately, though, I hesitantly scurried through the crowd in an effort to save myself sympathy offerings disguised as charity from those who carried the secrets of my romp through the Land of Unicorns. I felt like I was wearing a big "S" on my shirt like a scout badge, only one I wasn't proud of attaining. It stood for *Single*, or maybe just *Stupid*.

The sermon offered some comfort but there was always an end to the service, the next step, what to do or where to go. I didn't really care. I didn't even know. Every decision I faced seemed to end in wrong turns. I couldn't even figure out who I was, let alone what I wanted or where I wanted to spend my time. "This is gonna be a long road." I thought to myself.

Remembering the sermon today, I was certainly passionate, with many struggles. I surely felt the flames from that fire he was

79

talking about. Looking to my right and then my left, I saw nothing but empty chairs. Sure I had friends, but I couldn't help feeling as if I was missing a prince to share it all with, someone to dialogue after each message.

What good was a princess without a prince? I didn't have a castle or even a crown. The fact was, I had begun to believe I wasn't a princess at all anyway. I was a queen, the queen of failed relationships, that is. I had become accustomed to the struggle and didn't believe I deserved happiness anyway. Who would want to dialogue with that?

I wanted someone to love, at least that's what I kept telling myself. However deceived I may have been, it didn't make me seem so needy. Fact is, I *was* in need and frankly it was okay to need love in return. I desperately wanted that someone I loved to love me back, to pursue me, to want me, to leave no doubt. Was that asking too much? I wanted my Prince Charming to at least be willing to draw his sword.

I knew I didn't want someone any other way. I wanted to live openly and with an honesty that might have been lacking before. Truth always prevails, but the lack of it destroys hope. Personally I like brutal honesty. I can work with that. At least I would know where I stand and that ground isn't so shaky. I wanted someone to want me and accept me for *me*. This is the real me, like it or not.

It's like the famous quote, ***"If you can't love me at my worst, you don't deserve me at my best."*** Problem is, I wasn't even sure who I was. I remember hearing, *If you fail to find your identity in Christ, you will be vulnerable to accepting who others say you are.* I needed to find the truth about myself. How liberating it would be if I could find myself. Surely then I'd find my *Happily Even After.*

In the 1999 movie *Runaway Bride*, Maggi Carpenter, played by Julia Roberts, had already left three grooms at the altar. Having never discovered her own identity, she mirrored her fiancé's choices, preferring her eggs however they preferred theirs. Finally discovering she had an opinion of her own, she found the courage to stop running.

Runaway Bride

Was I the *Runaway Bride*? After all, I knew how I liked my eggs, didn't I? Truth is, I really didn't. I had grown so accustomed to being what I thought everyone wanted me to be, that I pretty much preferred any old egg, any old way and that went for the rest of my choices as well. I was living my life as if *my* choices didn't matter. Where had that thinking come from, and why was it acceptable?

The world was full of choices and I realized my need to start making a few of them for myself. Strange are the things you discover while trying to find yourself. Baskin Robbins has a few more than 36 flavors of ice cream now, and it's official, I'm still a *Cookies and Cream* girl. Soft drink flavors are limitless, and though Diet Coke is my poison, a splash of cherry flavoring couldn't hurt. I discovered over 43 different flavors of Lay's Potato Chips, but what exactly is a *Maui Onion* anyway?

No wonder it was so hard to make choices. The options were endless, and each came with an opportunity to mess things up. My choices never mattered, so why make the effort? I wasn't anyone special, so I'll just have what she's having. Except unlike Sally in, the 1989 movie, *When Harry Met Sally*, there wasn't as much pleasure in it for me... wink, wink.

M&M possibilities were numerous as the stars. Who even has enough time on their hands to figure it all out? There are plain, peanut, mint, almond, pretzel, rice crispy. All are covered in white, milk or dark chocolate, and the list goes on. However, I did discover the candy shell didn't keep its promise not to melt in our hands. More broken promises...

Chocolate always did make me feel better, so I went on a mission to find out, not only how I like my eggs, ice cream, soda and chips, but also how I like my M&Ms. So, let the testing begin! I never knew those little things held so much power. Something so trivial meant something so much greater that day. I found a little missing piece of myself and put it back where it belonged.

Once I started to look deep inside, my desires actually mattered, if only to me, and I was lifted to a whole new level of freedom. It was part of my healing process. Figuring out exactly what I desired from myself, others and life in general was a step in the direction of my *Happily Even After*. I was worth considering. Truly, for the first time in a very long time, I had considered myself in the grand scheme of things. Now if I could only find that other glass slipper, I'd be on top of the world.

I thought I'd already be on top of the world at this stage of the game. By now, I had been married for more than half of my life, and even if to two different princes, I was part of something important. I never pictured it any other way. It was where I placed my value, where I found purpose and meaning, however misplaced it was.

I didn't know how to be any other person. Finding that brave woman inside, the one who believed in herself, and could make it alone, was a must. She was hiding in there somewhere and I needed to coax her out. I would not likely survive this season of my life without her.

There was no other choice but to set out on a journey of self *re*-discovery. Who am I, really? What is it I'm truly seeking? I was the missing piece to be found, myself. I missed that step when starting out on my journey to *Happily Even After*. My fight was within *me*. Finding out whom I was first, then to find peace being *with* myself instead of being *by* myself.

That's what I'm really fighting for. It's up to me to receive the love, forgiveness and acceptance God offers. It is only when I know, love and accept who I am, that I can truly allow myself to be loved by another. When I can be content with or without, in feast or in famine, I can truly be satisfied with a partner. The bible tells us to be content.

"Not that I am speaking of being in need, for I have learned in whatever situation I am to be content." ~ Philippians 4:11

I needed to learn true contentment, to believe I was worthy. This meant fighting for myself through the challenges ahead. This is the fight I must win, in order to be truly content with or without my glass slipper. It is guaranteed to be a battle of great reward.

Winning the battle puts you on the right path. Without victory, my path took many twists and turns, returning to those same unwanted places. Everything there always looked so familiar, and not in a good way. "I give up, Lord." I cried out each time I circled the block. I was hoping for a better outcome as I went around one more time.

God knows I wanted to give up, but that would mean trusting God. When I told him I did, I was really saying, I *want* to, but I don't. True trust is taking the step forward when you can't see a thing in front of you. If I could see, how would that be trust? I had to stop trying to figure out what God was doing with my life. I had to give up control. "I trust You God." I said over and over, convincing myself if I said it out loud enough, maybe I would start to believe it.

I continued to plead as if God wasn't listening to me. "Why don't you just have Your way God?" I cried out. "You're sovereign, God, why don't you just do it? Have *Your* way!" It was as if I now believed God needed the convincing. Once again, almost audibly, I heard. "I am. You just don't like *My* way." That was a powerful message from the Holy Spirit.

Once again I was speechless. I could see no other choice than to let go. Giving up didn't mean failure. Rather, it was a success story. I hadn't been successful with anything else I had tried to accomplish on my own. This time was no different. I wasn't giving up so much as giving *it* up, and all that meant.

I had to trust Him with what He was, and was *not,* doing with my life. I knew He was either saving me *from* something, or saving me *for* something, but I was being saved for sure and only He could do that. I knew it was the only way I was going to find true *Happily Even After*.

I knew in giving it up there would be no *take backs*. Every time before, when He felt distant, I went back on my word. I started to feel invisible to everyone around me, even God. I was surrounded by people and felt completely alone. I sank deeper, but every time I got to that desperate place, God would send a reminder that He saw me.

He didn't judge me for continually snatching back the trust I had placed in His hands. He saw my tears, heard my cries and felt my pain. He could relate to sorrow and rejection. Once again, I knew I was held and loved. I knew the Lover of my soul understood and had compassion for me. God *did* see me, and He knew what I was going through. I was the apple of His eye.

"...whatever touches you, touches the apple of His eye."
Zechariah 2:8

What may have looked unfamiliar to me was ultra-clear to the God who designed the path especially for me. Maybe it was time to follow the *designer* path. I've tried it my way, and that didn't end happily after anything.

I would have to muster all the energy I had to live my life with joy. I not only had to let go, but find strength to continue climbing this mountain, find contentment in the climb, and hang on until I reached the top. It wouldn't be easy but steadfastness promised a great reward.

"And let steadfastness have its full effect, that you may be perfect and complete, lacking in nothing." James 1:4 ESV

The only way I would lack nothing was to put my faith into action. It would be my cross to bear.

~ There is a distinct possibility that I am profoundly and irreversibly screwed up. ~
Runaway Bride

Chapter Thirteen

~ *The Cross Bearer* ~

We all bear crosses. Some bear them on strong, and steady backs while some balance them on the backs of others. Some crosses are heavy and some light but one thing is true, cross bearers suffer from the weight of the cross they carry, no matter the size. In order to carry its weight we must be greater than the cross itself. We must become greater than what we suffer in order to conquer it. There was only one way to do that, fight for it.

He who is in you is greater than he who is

in the world." ~ 1 John 4:4

Not a fan of conflict, I wanted everything handed to me without a fight, without a challenge. God designed most of what was worth fighting for, worth the fight. I was wrestling with the enemy and it was a fight to win the prize. No matter what I was facing, He was in the ring with me, fighting my battle Himself. The hurt was all still fresh to me.

My word of the year became *surreal.* It was the only word I found that could describe how I felt. It's not a life I wanted or planned for and it certainly wasn't the place for the woman I wanted to be. That woman had a companion, one that she trusted to accept everything that defined her.

She was strong, confident and knew she was destined for greatness. But, I was nothing like that. I was weak and waiting on someone to rescue me. Not just someone but *the* one who found me worthy. I didn't even care that the scale I was using to measure my worthiness was so deeply flawed.

I had messed up so much I didn't deserve to have a life full of joy. I acted as if I had to earn God's favor. Did I really deserve the chances God always gave me? I could never be worthy enough to receive God's favor and mercy, not without the blood of Jesus. I needed His mercy and forgiveness, but I also needed to forgive myself. I had faith, though my actions showed otherwise.

"Faith by itself, without works is dead." ~ James 2:17 ESV

My faith was on death row. I was making a declaration of a truth I desperately wanted to possess but feared I didn't. I said I'd have courage. I said I'd trust, but I truly no longer even believed, so my faith *was* presumed dead. I couldn't follow His direction, or maybe it's just that I wouldn't.

My pride and selfishness were the works that came out from the *Me* that needed saving. I hated that. "Please remove that girl from me." I begged. "and replace her with someone who is beautiful to this world, not in a superficial way but in a world changing kinda way."

I knew with all my dirtiness I was still beautiful to Him, but I didn't reflect much light covered in mud. My hope, in my insufficiency, was that He would shine through all my brokenness. Every crack and every chip revealed a place where He had worked the hardest on me. Always repairing, constantly rebuilding yet never giving up. He loved me. He loves me, and always will. He has the scars to prove it.

Knowing and believing this truth revealed the answer to that first and most difficult question I had presented to myself...*Who Am I?* Each season of my life is showing me more and more of who I really am. Some things I liked and some things I disliked. I learned that I'm a little stronger than I thought, a little weaker than I want to be, and I'm completely normal.

Tragedies cause us to overflow with whatever is on the inside, the substance of who we truly are. It's where we find bits of strength, weakness, fear, doubt, anxiety, passion, forgiveness, regret and the list goes on, but it can all come pouring out at once when we're tested. My mother-in-law use to say, *When you bump a glass, what's in it spills out,* and she was right.

I ran on an energy fueled by passion and a zeal for life that flows through my very core. When something upset that flow, it was physically and emotionally painful. I grabbed onto what I thought would make the pain go away. It's only natural, but I wasn't quite sure if what I grabbed onto was capable of keeping the pain away for long. I was encouraged to let God alone take it, but my flesh was weak.

I must fight to rest in God's hands, to just be. How do I accomplish that? Can I truly be happy just being still? I've always had a plan, always protecting my heart with my own plans. Why did I feel it needed protecting? Do I need to change or is it too late? Will there be another chance?

I may never find answers to the questions I seek, but the older I get, the less I need them. Realizing who I am was something that I needed to define in order to find my true *Happily Even After.*

I knew I was loved unconditionally. God said I was, **"...fearfully and wonderfully made."** I was the ***apple of His eye***. He even counted every hair on my head, and knew me by name. He knew me when I was in my mother's womb, and there was no doubt, He also knew the parts of me no one else could see. Yet, He still loved me, had a good plan for my life and I could be confident that He who had begun a good work in me would complete it. All I had to do was believe it and receive it. Why was that so hard?

I was looking for someone with a suit of armor, one carrying a lost slipper, riding a white horse and calling out my name. I don't know why I gave him such great power. The real strength was finding myself among all the glitz and glamour of the fairy tale life I was searching for.

As I sat alone, I saw a glimpse of *me,* the girl in the mirror, the one I had abandoned long ago. I was sure she still had a chance, if she could remember that she was everything she was made to be. It was inside her all along. Now if she could hold onto that.

Who Am I?

I am a forgiven and accepted child of the living God.

I am what He wills me to be, with every failure and flaw.

I am what I profess, and what I profess not, to be.

I am what I am whether you like or dislike me.

I am the sum of the choices I make and the ones I decline...

The chances I take and those I leave behind.

I am what I appear to be and what I hide from sight.

I am what I do and say in the dark and in the light.

I'm the one on Facebook, Twitter and Instagram for all the world to see.

And I am the photo on the cutting room floor, those viewed only by me

I am His alone with nothing of value to bring

He accepts me just as I am, for I am a child of the Living King.

Completely undeserved, He took me out of my hopelessness and gave me a life worth living. Now all I had to do was live in such a way that my Prince Charming would see *me*, the real flawed me and still want me. He would at least know what he was getting. No additions or substitutions were available. It was a "no special orders" kind of deal, and there was no exchange policy.

This agreement came with my commitment and one was completely expected in return. There were potholes, not loopholes. There would be *ups and downs* but no *down and outs*. No valley was too wide nor mountain too steep with this kind of commitment. There was promise of a shared reward because everyone would benefit from our success.

Protecting that union at all costs became, not only our responsibility, but our family's and friend's as well. Finding the one who would be willing to join into this agreement or commitment was difficult, much more difficult as the years passed.

Once again I borrowed the shoulder of a friend. His advice always meant a lot. "Not sure what to say really, other than there has to be more satisfying things to do to bring you true fulfillment." He added, "Maybe you should focus on anything and everything except finding someone for now."

It wasn't rocket science and nothing he said was unfamiliar, but he had a way of telling me exactly what I needed to hear and his timing was perfect. His honest advice hit home. I was scared to admit it, but was ready to begin. So, I recommitted myself to focusing on helping others, finding a cause and giving myself away to something that would bring true fulfillment.

On my knees, I asked for guidance and clarity and made a decision that would prove to be one of the most truly fulfilling things in a long time. There were always ministries within the church, mission trips, and other programs chomping at the bit for a fresh volunteer. But I found the, *one-on-one* needs of broken women beckoning me to share my pain, feel theirs, and let our tears swirl into a puddle of fresh healing.

There really *were* more fulfilling things to do in life other than focus on the past and what I had lost. I stood to gain so much more if I put myself on the right path. I began filling my down time searching for more broken spirits. Together, we were much stronger than we were apart. Our shared struggles lessoned the pain and increased the joy.

Sadly there was still one heartbreaking piece of the puzzle that remained elusive. I still longed for someone to share these experiences. Although they were rewarding, I wanted to be rewarded as *we*, not just *me*. It was clear from the beginning that God intended for us to find a partner. God created male and female of every species and none of them were expected to do life without the other. No wonder I was feeling incomplete.

Since I hadn't found a suitable partner, I had to forget about armor, white horses and slippers for a while. I needed to become the woman God intended me to be. Love isn't about finding the right person, but about being the right person, and I wanted to be the right person. Since I was so stubborn, that could take a lifetime.

I had to be ready to accept the fact that I may spend the rest of my life alone, but there was no *Happily Even After* there. At least that's what I had been taught as a little girl. I had no reason to question all those fairy tales. Conspiring against me, they all promised the same happiness, so I believed it. I just didn't want to get to the end of my journey and find that I had pined away for someone who didn't exist.

I believed by now I would be walking through life with a like-minded, like-hearted man, one who cared to hold my hand as much as I cared to hold his. I wanted to look back at our footprints in the sand and see that during the hardest times, they drew closer together, not further apart. When there was only one set, his were alternating with mine, as we carried each other through the difficult seasons of life as God had carried us.

It seemed like a fairy tale, but I knew if others had made it a reality, it too could be mine. I was surrounded by these kinds of fairy tales. They were everywhere, except here, with me. If there was still time to live *Happily Even After* at this stage, I needed and longed for a sign to prove it.

"God, what am I supposed to do?" I asked. "Would you give me a sign? If I am to be the other half of someone, why have I not met that someone yet?" Then I said, "I will wait on You, God, if you'll just give me a sign."

The Holy Spirit stopped me before I got the words out, and ever so gently responded. "Sweet child, you are right. You *will* wait. How you choose to do so is completely up to you."

The point was well taken, and my countenance almost immediately changed. Waiting, as I said earlier, was not my specialty. I knew the Lord was going to grow me in this area, and keep growing me until I finally stopped resisting. It's in the *wait* that we grow up and I guess I felt a little taller that day.

"Okay God, You win." I said, as if I had been in competition with Him. I thought I could out think, out do and out plan God. He's a sovereign God. At the very least, I *thought* I knew what He would want for me. Even when my ideals were honorable, His ideal for my life took a very different form.

He has it all figured out if I would move out of the way. He is a gentleman who won't force His way in, although He is always pressing in to remind me of His love. He has all I need wrapped up in His word. He promised to direct my path.

"Trust in the Lord with all your heart and lean not onto your own understanding. In all your ways acknowledge Him and He will direct your paths." Proverbs 3:5-6

He promises to give us the desires of our hearts.

"Commit your ways to the Lord and He shall give you the desires of your heart." Psalm 37:4

He promises to work all things out for our good.

"God causes all things to work together for good to those who love Him and are called according to His purpose."

Romans 8:28

His promises are infinite. God promised that I would be rewarded much, if I was faithful with a little.

"Whoever can be faithful with the few, can also be faithful with much..." Luke 16:10

Was this the way I was to be rewarded after I had been so faithful? It didn't feel like much of a reward to me. I asked myself, *Is it over? Am I done? Am I gonna die?* Yes, but apparently not today.

I was still young and even if I didn't have a whole lifetime ahead of me, God certainly had enough time to reward me with much if He willed. Then, in my solitude and there on my knees, it occurred to me, He already had.

He can withhold anything He wants from my life if it stands in the way of His will. I had a slight suspicion that until I could focus on what God wanted for my life, He wasn't going to trust me with anyone else. When I can fix my heart and mind on Him, while sharing a piece of it with someone special, maybe He'd actually trust me with that special one.

I knew God had a plan for my life. I was just anxious to get His plan going *my* way. But, I was determined, once again, to fix my gaze upon the one whom I trusted with my future. I realized then that there had always been a profound calling on my life. It was placed in me when I was conceived and it hadn't changed.

I was called to love God and to love others. My purpose was clear, to love Him and lead people to Him, with, or without, Prince Charming. I didn't need anything special to do that.

There was no need to attain a certain level of success or a certain position in life before God would use me. He was just taking His time, molding me and preparing me for it. His plan was on course, even if I wasn't. Just because I chose my steps, however detoured, His plan had never taken one, and all He wanted me to do was let Him work.

It occurred to me, the purpose He had called me to just might require me to be alone. I might never be able to accomplish it with my focus on a Mr. Right or even Mr. Worth The Risk. There might be something specific I was called to do requiring my total focus, my whole heart and all of my attention. God knew my nature and He knew my focus would be on the fairy tale and not the mission for which I was called.

Tired of carrying this cross, I couldn't help but ask God do something to make me feel better in the meantime. "You command the universe!" I cried out. "Couldn't you just give me someone to love?" He gave Joe to Linda and John to Joan. Was I any different?

My mom and dad weren't Cinderella and Prince Charming, but their life was no less a fairy tale to them. They had their challenges. I could only hear their drama from a distance, but I remember being afraid at times.

They managed, with divine intervention, to remain steadfast when it came to their *Happily Even After*, and to this day show the world true unconditional love. Their story brings hope to me. It began in no extraordinary way. Just two ordinary young kids still full of dreams.

~ *"Dispose thyself to patience rather than to comfort, and to the bearing of the cross rather than gladness."* ~
Thomas 'a Kempis

Chapter Fourteen

~ *The Princess And The Colonel* ~

On February 28, 1941 God delivered my mom, Robbie Lee Mason to a wonderful couple by the name of Ollie Cleo Morgan and Robert Lee Mason. Her Aunt Bithey told her as a teenager she was the ugliest and hairiest baby she had ever seen. The teenage years are extraordinarily difficult and a bit awkward, and Aunt B. did her part to rob her niece of any self-esteem she may have.

Mom was as skinny as a rail, and those years didn't go so well for her. Little did she know her luck was about to change for the better. She set out on her journey and her fairy tale began quite by accident.

One bus ride at just the right moment, with just the right guy seated strategically behind her, and my mom's life would change forever. Was it fate that brought two 16 year-old kids together? Was it fantasy or was it a fairy tale?

I don't know but this had the makings of a *Happily Ever After* if any chance meeting did. Unlike the princess in, *The Princess and the Pea* fairy tale, mom's test would come in the form of a colonel. Lieutenant Colonel, James H. Jinks Jr., my dad.

He was wearing blue jeans with his cuffs rolled up, and a peach shirt. If that wasn't enough to catch mom's attention, the Penny Loafers, with real pennies in them, was. "That was hot back then." She remembers.

Dad was quite the class clown and knew just how to get the attention of one skinny, insecure gal who was on the bus that day.

She was sitting in front of him, and he could think of no easier way than to steal the hairpins right out of her ponytail. Way to go dad! Without a second thought, she turned around and stole his ink pen out of his shirt pocket. It was the only fair thing to do and she refused to give it back for a very long time. Must be where I get that sass.

Jimbo, as mom fondly referred to him, worked as a bag boy in the local Setzer's grocery store where her Mom and Dad shopped. She recognized him as the boy from the school bus, and he happened to be bagging their groceries that day. His Dad was in line in front of them.

Mom was wearing a yellow ribbon around her neck and dad couldn't contain himself as he whistled the song, *around her neck she wore a yellow ribbon*. Loud and clear, it could be heard throughout the store. "I was so embarrassed." mom cried, "I couldn't wait to get out of there."

It was just a few weeks after that chance meeting when she boarded another bus. This time it was a bus to the city's annual Veteran's Day Parade, and to mom's delight, dad appeared, and let destiny take its course. The seat next to her was calling his name, so he took it in anticipation of their first unexpected date. He asked her if he could watch the parade with her and she said yes. He had stolen her hairpins, he had stolen the seat next to her, and now he was stealing her heart.

My mom invited him to come to church with her the next Sunday and, without hesitation, Dad said yes. She coughed through the whole service that night, and thought he probably couldn't wait for it to be over. However, Prince Charming was hoping for the opposite. Reassuring her, he took her hand and held it tightly. She felt warm and cared for. His attempts to impress this Cinderella worked.

Dad was on the high school track team and in the Senior Chorus so he stayed after school for practices, seldom able to take the bus home. School bus rides were never so much fun before mom joined the scene and he hated missing out on time with her. It made it all the more challenging to find ways to be together.

They started *going steady*, as they called it. She wore his class ring on a chain around her neck, a ritual reserved for only the most special relationships. They had planned to get married in the spring of that year, but soon after receiving his diploma, dad enlisted in the United States Army. Their wedding would be postponed until he returned home on leave in December after attending Officer Candidate School.

Three years after watching that parade together, they exchanged vows in their home church in Jacksonville, Florida Dec 22, 1959 and began their *Happily Even After* journey together. As naive young people, they didn't know their future would be an uphill climb, and that was just the beginning.

Shortly after he graduated from Officer Candidate School, dad was assigned to Ft. Sill, Oklahoma where Judy, their first daughter, my only sibling, was born on Oct 6, 1960. They were just a normal military family, moving from one assignment to another. From Ft. Sill, Oklahoma, Ft. Rucker, Alabama, Ft. Benning, Georgia, to Sembach Army Base and Mannheim Army Base, both in Germany. They never knew where their country would ask them to serve, but Mom knew no matter where it sent her Prince Charming, she would be right there beside him.

Days were long at times. Being a new wife, with a new child, in a new city was a little scary to mom as a young woman. She felt confident that if her knight in shining armor could lead an army, literally, he was capable of leading her and her daughter safely.

Not long after, they relocated to Ft. Rucker, Alabama for Dad to attend Flight School, their second daughter Kathie, (that's me) was born on January 23, 1962. Life was little more than routine until four years later when they found themselves in Germany. It was their first time that far from home, clear across the ocean.

The uphill climb continued shortly after dad's first assignment to Germany began. Mom was called home at the sudden death of her mother. It was extremely difficult being a young mother in another country, traveling hundreds of miles away leaving her two little girls behind. Nevertheless, she and dad boarded a plane and headed back stateside to bid farewell to my grandma Ollie.

The Princess and the Colonel

After spending a year in Germany, dad loaded us up once again and headed for home. It was a welcome relief to mom. Though the military had a close-knit circle of support, there was nothing like the support of real family, and support was what she needed now more than ever.

Mom quickly found no amount of support would be enough to ease the fears that were just around the corner. Dad would now be going on a tour of duty unlike any other before. The orders to go to war would come complete with a country that didn't support the war at all, or the men who would be called to fight it. They had hit an all-time low.

Vietnam. It was 1966 and a very trying time for our country and an even harder time for marriages and families all over the nation. Fathers were taken away from their families and women were left with childrearing and solely caring for the needs of the family.

The *Commander In Chief* had requested his military to serve their country with honor. She was asked to say goodbye to her Prince Charming, watch him walk away not for a few days, not even for a few months but a year or longer and without the guarantee of a return.

Dad not only served a tour of duty in Vietnam, he served two. "It was really tough on us while he was away from home." Mom remembers. "We thrived on the times that we could just hear the sound of his voice by radio."

"Hello daddy, over." We would say as one waited anxiously after the other. "Hello baby girl, over", dad would respond. And just about the time you were able to say hello, time was up and you were forced to say goodbye again. There was no end to the line of anxious soldiers waiting to hear the voices of loved ones, if only for a moment.

"It ripped away a piece of my heart every single time I was forced to pull the receiver out of each of their tightly clutched fingers." Mom recalls. We looked forward to the mail, just hoping to get a letter from him." Sometimes we would get lucky and receive a cassette tape with a recorded message.

Choices were limited during times of war to what the country and the military allowed. Taking one day at a time, we marked each one slowly off the calendar, just doing what we had to do. Times

Times were rough, and would have rocked any Cinderella's world, but mom was a determined woman who had become strong and resolved to support her man in the thick of it all. It's in these times that relationships are strengthened or torn apart. My parents proved that the strongest of bonds can be made through great struggle and that sacrifice is not only essential, but rewarding as well.

They were no stranger to struggle and sacrifice and by this time had only been married for 11 of their 56 years together. Much more struggle and sacrifice was to come and after one more assignment to Mannheim, Germany in 1972 and 1973 they moved back to their hometown to begin a *normal* life together.

There would be no threat of war, at least not overseas. But, heaviness weighed upon Dad's heart and mind. He would now fight a war within himself to keep his family provided for, and to be the knight in shining armor his Cinderella had fought to support all those years.

Leaving the U.S. Army dad had proudly served for so many years as an officer was life altering for him and my mother. The road he decided to take next would be a sacrifice mom would be challenged to make with him.

Making the decision to leave your daughters in one country to stay beside your husband while he is 3000 miles away in another is equally life altering. How does one make this decision and how does one make it without hesitation or regret? The answer is, they don't.

My mom was thrown into the land of *what ifs*. What if people talk? What if something happens to me, to us? What if something happens to them? She had to think of more positive alternatives if she wanted to support her Prince. After all, love is a sacrifice and you can't please everyone, so she changed her perspective. What if everything *did* work out? What if this **is** the best decision for the wellbeing of my husband and family? What if this *is* God's plan?

With that, mom made the decision to follow my dad to Jeddah, Saudi Arabia where he would be piloting a jet for some of the most decorated foreign leaders. Not only did she agree to follow in support, but would be moving to a country that didn't place much value on her role as a woman in business or society in general. It was a scary place, completely unfamiliar, and they learned to keep close the things they valued and those they loved.

Many things had to be put in motion for this transition to work smoothly for the whole family, so mom made a list and went to work. An older college student was hired as a roommate, letters to church leaders and school officials were sent, and family and friends were given fair warning that two concerned parents would be enlisting their eyes and ears.

Leaving her girls was one of the toughest decisions of mom's life and with it she would paint a picture of true love and sacrifice. She always believed she was giving her girls a gift with this lesson. At the age of 16, the idea that mom and dad loved each other, and us, deepened in me. Dad showed it by providing and mom showed it by loving in spite of the circumstances. She trusted God to take care of us. After all, He loved us more than she did.

It didn't come without ridicule though, and it didn't come without reservation, but it did come with a confidence and a faith in God and her husband. Dad knew what he was doing for the sake of his family, even if others didn't agree or even understand. They opened up a whole new world for me and my sister, and we were a part of something not many young people can even dream of. With all the lessons included, their seven-year stay proved to be one of our family's greatest experiences.

Once they returned home, life took another drastic turn. Dad went to work for a major airline company, but after 10 years as a professional commercial pilot, had to undergo open-heart surgery. A quadruple bypass stood in the way of a second chance. Although a scary endeavor, it was nonetheless necessary.

Dad became aware that this would ultimately retire him from the airlines. He had flown all of his life, fresh out of high school. It was in his DNA and wasn't prepared to give it up, but it wasn't an option. So, he said goodbye to a lifelong passion and together with mom embarked on a new journey to fulfill a lifelong dream. Or so they thought...

Owning and running a fish camp, and riverfront restaurant may have seemed like a dream come true. But, once they had received the keys to Sunset Landing in Welaka, Florida, their dream became a nightmare.

The name painted a picture of beautiful evenings sitting on the porch of your cabin, sipping sweet iced tea, while watching the sun set into an amazing orange haze. Only, they weren't the ones sitting on the porch, but the ones serving those who were privileged enough to do so.

They were no strangers to hard work. Their determination went far beyond that of their worn out equipment. Aged pilings and sinking docks were drowning underneath the weight of fishing gear and ice chests, damaged by years of family fun, and a never-ending list of unfinished renovations awaited the sound of Dad's toolbox opening.

Days were long, and the bed in their deteriorating mobile home was rarely visited. It was quite a shock leaving the prosperity of a beautiful home, manicured lawn and jobs that provided financial satisfaction. The days of finding rest on their patio with a glass of wine and a good book became a memory.

If two people could make this work though, it was my parents, and they did, for 7 years, together. They cleaned bathrooms, sold bait and tackle, and had the best *Lunker Burger* anywhere in town. Robbie fried fish and her famous corn fritters, as she rented cabins and pontoon boats. It was tough, but there was an understanding. Neither preferred an easier life if it meant doing it without the other.

It became more difficult on mom physically. There was a cost and the piper was ready to be paid. The stress of the last 7 years took its toll on her health as well, and mom underwent a pacemaker implant. Both of their surgeries had been successful, giving them a chance to start over, but that meant one more move for this *Happily Even After* story.

Everyone in the family knew the time would come when the two of them could no longer sustain the kind of grueling effort it took to keep things running. The family was overjoyed to see them load up the truck and move to what would be there home for the next 15 plus years. We were excited for them to start this new season of refreshing and relaxation. They had earned it.

It was a beautiful, vibrant, and active community for *young at heart* seniors. They would meet some of their best friends, play some of their best golf and remember what it means to be truly committed to each other.

They have been through the best of times and the worst of times right there in that spot. Finding their love and sacrifice had carried them through disappointment, loss, and tragedy, but growing their faith and courage to face whatever came next.

Mom said, "Our happiness and joy outweigh our times of sorrow. These last 56 plus years, including those before we were married, were full of uphill climbs." Mom and dad fought wars on every side, but fought them together.

They were blessed with a great family. Neither was perfect, and it was the toughest, most painful yet rewarding assignment they had ever taken. The reward came in a legacy that would be handed down to the next generation.

Mom beams as she talks about her family. Following in her footsteps, we have learned to be faithful women of God who follow our hearts, and live in service to others. She is proud of Judy's accomplishments as a registered nurse, being full of God's grace and mercy. And of me, an entrepreneur and musician sharing the gift of music to glorify and honor God. She and dad always did boast of their girls.

We are proud that both mom and dad taught us to love God, and raise our children and grandchildren in the nurture and admonition of the Lord. God has blessed us. With four terrific grandchildren and five precious great grandchildren, they have plenty left to do.

My parents retired in the Villages, Florida, *"the friendliest hometown,"* only a couple of hours from family. "It just doesn't get any better than this," Mom finished.

They serve the Lord in their local church and dad has a honey-do list a mile long. Ladies in the village consider him their honey as well. Probably because he is the cheapest handy man in town, and can literally fix anything. Mom doesn't mind, though. "It gets him out of the house, and spending too much time together can be dangerous," mom says with a laugh.

She is a *Past Regent*, and active member of both the DAR (Daughters of the American Revolution) and the UDC. (United Daughters of the Confederacy) She left me with these words:

"During these last 56 years of marriage we have had our share of ups and downs. There have been times of joy, happiness, sorrow and pain throughout our journey. We have lost many of our friends and loved ones on both sides of the family. The only constant thing in our life was our Lord. He gave us strength and abilities that we had no idea we could pull out of ourselves when we needed it."

At one point in my life, I screamed at God and asked him "How much more do you want from me? What do you want me to do? I heard just one word, Persevere."

Dad enjoys playing golf and tinkering with just about anything but what he really enjoys are the relationships he has built with fellow veterans and pilots. They spend time swapping war stories with their hero brothers and find a sense of accomplishment and healing in each one.

At the age of 76, he continues his love of flying at a nearby flying club. He has been recognized for his aircraft readiness skills and was asked to be safety officer for the club. He takes great pride in that, especially since recently taking his grandkids, great-grand kids and his 79 year-young Sister on their first *Free flight* adventure, Dad piloting, of course. Beyond serving his country, this has been the pinnacle of his flying career, creating smiles and memories they won't soon forget.

He erected a windsock at the airport for every pilot to use and enjoy for many years. It's as constant and steadfast as the man I call Dad, un-movable, and a reminder of his continued sacrifice for those he loves and serves. A permanent plaque was placed at its base in honor of his generous donation. It reads:

FREEFLIGHT AIRPORT

2FA6

Frank and Yvonne Arenas, Owners

This windsock was produced, erected and donated by

LTC. James H. Jinks Jr. USA (Ret.)

24 March, 2015

"May you always have fair winds and blue skies."

Theirs was a great story. I wanted to love that way. When I said, *I love you* I wanted it to mean something more, something passionate, wild and extravagant. I wanted it to be extraordinary and contagious.

"I have died everyday waiting for you. I have loved you for a thousand years and I'll love you for a thousand more." ~

1000 years ~ Christina Perri & David Hodges

Where was that kind of love? Some say it's only in fairy tales but I refused to believe it didn't exist. This is one time when I hoped that life *did* imitate art. Someone had to write those scripts, those songs and that gave me hope. There had to be a love out there worth dying for.

I am quite certain that mom and dad are very grateful that they stood on their faith in God, and their love and commitment to each other as they can now see where their fight changed the world and their family's world forever.

"The Legacy"

We rarely get to hear or read about how our parents met and fell in love. Often times our parents keep their stories to themselves, especially their struggles. Maybe they fear we will see failure and think less of them.

It has been a blessing to write the love story of Jim and Robbie Jinks, my mom and dad. Hearing about their journey, their successes, AND failures have made them more genuinely and authentically human, and made me more grateful than ever for them. They give us all hope for our own fairy tale, found in the valley at times.

A "legacy" is, by definition, 'a gift'. It refers to something someone leaves you when they pass from this life to the next. My parents are still here with us and a gift to all who know them. But, when they leave this earth, their "legacy" is the beautiful love story, and honorable life they've lived serving God, their country, and their family. They have been, and continue to be, a true gift to me and our family.

I will forever be grateful for their steadfast and unconditional love for each other and their girls. They show us a great example of the covenant, living out their Happily Even After. They taught us to persevere through every trial, seek God and never give up. I can't think of a better way to honor them than to share them with you.

Thank you Mom and Dad,

Your loving daughter,

Kathie

"A Promise Kept"

I think the greatest legacy two people can leave the next generation is not one of material wealth, but one of faith and trust that begins with a "Promise Kept". When we marry, we all make a promise to love, honor and cherish each other in sickness and health, for richer or poorer, for better or worse as long as we both shall live. My mom and dad began their journey with that promise and it has been tested by time and distance. I remain inspired by their enduring love and devotion to each other through the roller coaster ride of life. A promise kept is like a seed planted in the soil and through the droughts of lack, wind storms that tossed them from place to place, torrential rains of loss and tears and sunshine of great victories and joys along the way. Nourished by a determination to press on, a tree was planted, "A Family Tree", with roots that are strong and stretch deep into the earth creating a strong foundation. I've witnessed the good times and the bad, and have watched them hold fast to a promise that was made so many years ago. I cannot think of anything more valuable to leave to the next generation, which are "The branches". Each branch stretches out from their center and touches the world around them. They were born out of faith, love and a "Promise Kept".

Thank you Mom and Dad.
Your loving daughter,

Judy

Jim & Robbie Jinks

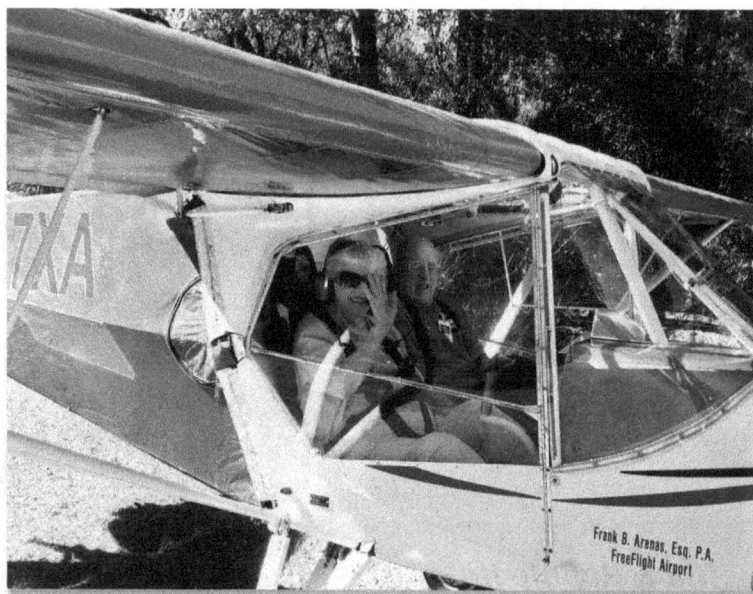

Frank B. Arenas, Esq. P.A.
FreeFlight Airport

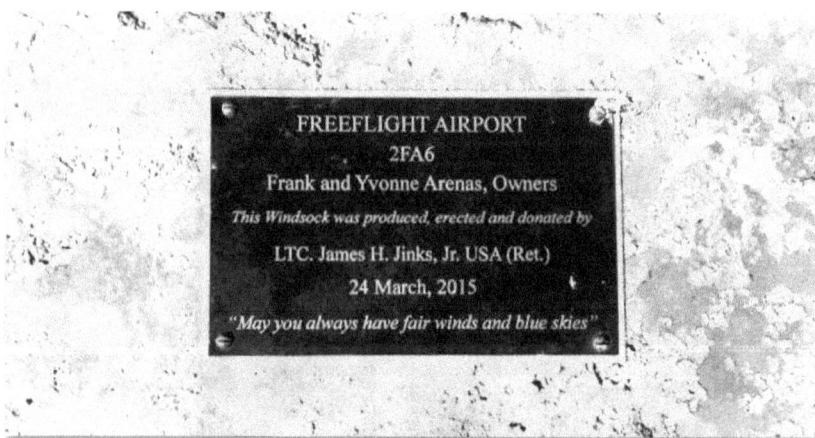

FREEFLIGHT AIRPORT
2FA6
Frank and Yvonne Arenas, Owners
This Windsock was produced, erected and donated by
LTC. James H. Jinks, Jr. USA (Ret.)
24 March, 2015
"May you always have fair winds and blue skies"

Chapter Fifteen

~ *Island Of Misfits* ~

Sometimes God asks you to do something extraordinary. It doesn't seem extraordinary at the time. It may even seem routine or mundane. Now I would take slow and unsure steps in a direction I didn't choose for myself.

I sensed somehow, this was the direction to a better plan. So, I prayed for the strength to follow through, and the faith to believe that when His plan was completed, I would see the mundane become extraordinary.

I wanted the extraordinary for myself. Every fairy tale could be this way, but in reality, in a world that has turned its heart away from God, stories like these are few and far between. It takes a whole lot of intestinal fortitude to love the way God commanded.

"You shall love the Lord your God with all your heart and with all your soul and with all your strength and with all your mind, and your neighbor as yourself." Luke 10:27

I wasn't ready to spend my life alone. I enjoyed being alone at times, but being *alone*, alone, that was a different story altogether. A shared life meant joy and sorrow were shared. A partner in those moments meant miraculously joy would be doubled and pain divided. But when those moments came for me now, I could find no one there. I wasn't sure what scared me more, being alone, or being with someone and still feeling alone.

Where's that strong person residing inside all of this flesh and bone? All I had to do was find the strength to take one more step. If I just kept going, I would eventually end up somewhere else. Anywhere seemed better than here. Was this God's will? What was He asking of me?

There next to me was the Word of God and it was opened to the same verse I had read many times before.

"He sticks closer than a brother". Proverbs 18:24

God was close and would stick by me through all of those moments. He not only doubled my joy, He multiplied it. He not only divided my pain, He wiped it away. He didn't just want me to survive it. He wanted me to conquer it. Chances of victory with Him, were much greater than without Him.

Like a roller coaster, my life was scary, nauseating, and wildly entertaining. With each turn, I got back in line to spend another hour waiting for the chance to experience the two-minute thrill all over again. But, this part of my story would prove to be the most terrifying ride of them all, online dating.

When I was young, this service was reserved for the lonely, divorced, the un-chosen few from the Island of Misfits. It wasn't for people like me, even if I did now fit the profile. That was a sad revelation in itself. I attempted to sign up for an online account on several occasions, but stopped short of hitting the *submit* button.

I kept giving myself one excuse after the other why I shouldn't be doing this. Every time I'd get to the last step, I'd close my laptop before the tears could soak the keyboard. The promise of more rejection was not what I had in mind.

"Everyone does it now." My friend assured me. "It's the safest way to meet people these days." I was waiting to actually believe it, I suppose. So, after several attempts, with fear and trembling, I finally hit submit.

I felt like a loser, and as tears filled my eyes once again, I was flung into the world of endless profile filtering, among all the other misfits, just like me.

It was a scary place full of men I didn't recognize and certainly didn't know. I wasn't even sure I wanted to know any of them. None of their profiles told their real story. I knew at this age, their faces would reveal the pain of a thousand disappointments, but pictures represented them inaccurately.

Messages flooded in, not because I was a great catch, but I was the newest fish in the ocean of millions. The thought of returning one of them felt daunting and I found myself paralyzed to respond. I couldn't click the *turn off chat* button quick enough.

Each one had a list of requirements. They were all looking for *some*thing, or *one* thing. I didn't want to give myself away to anyone who didn't want the whole package. I was looking for someone who believed in a passionate, lifelong love affair with *all* of me. Anything less seemed like a friendly courtesy.

Courtesy means, *well-mannered and polite*, definitely not what I was looking for. I was hoping for a raw and un-mannered wild love affair that would last a lifetime, if that was even attainable.

I wanted something real, something tangible yet intangible as well. I was one girl, one real, flawed, hopeless, yet committed girl. I wanted one guy, one real, flawed, hopeless, yet committed guy. He had to want all of me, the whole package, every wrinkle and every scar. I longed for someone who believed in *"long, slow, deep, wet kisses that lasted three days."* Like Crash Davis quotes in the 1988 movie, Bull Durham.

I wanted someone to take me *forever*, not just take me out. I longed to share life with someone who wanted to take his time, and mine, then give it all back again. I didn't want to take care of a man, raise a man, or train a man, as if I could. I did, however, want a man that was trained by God to take care of himself so we could take care of each other. I deserved that and so did he.

After searching through what seemed like thousands of profiles, I began to cry again. It was becoming clear to me that my waterproof mascara was going to fulfill its true purpose in my life. This was one of those less than magical moments that caused me pain and I was giving it permission to steal away more of my time than I ever wanted. Even still, I couldn't help but ask myself, *how did I get here?*

Would I find my rescuer here? My thought was, only if I wanted the guy who's profile was a snapshot of him picking his nose, now that's charming. Or the one suitor that was clever enough to show us his rooster on a leash. Maybe it would be the one who, though his profile said he was young and active, looked like grandpa from the Beverly Hillbillies. (No offense to grandpa)

Funny thing is, there was someone just right for all three of those guys, some sweet, blushing lady on the other side of her computer looking at his profile saying, "My hero." Seemed like there was someone for everyone, except me.

I couldn't figure out whether I truly wanted to meet guys, or whether I was just angry. Maybe if I found someone to fill the void in my life, it would make me feel valuable, however wrong that may be. In my sheltered world of work – church - home, I wasn't likely to meet someone any other way. The bar scene was scarier than online dating and really wasn't my thing, so what other options were there?

I began to realize that I had never dated. I married right after high school. After that marriage failed, I married my next husband too quickly never experiencing this scary world of dating. I knew how to be married, but I sure didn't know how to play the dating game, nor did I want to learn. It looked from the outside like more rejection and pain. That was not a road I wanted to go down as a teenager, and I hadn't changed my mind as an adult.

The Island of Misfits was no place for me. It was cold, lonely and scary. But, even the abominable snowman was trainable, and the misfits did in fact save Christmas. They did it together as a team. They had each other, and this was a thread I seemed to be missing.

Everyone had someone. That's the way it's supposed to be, right? Where was my other half? I lived under the misconception I had spent the majority of my life living as half an equation. When I was subtracted from that equation I continued to grasp at anything and everything that would put it all back together the way I recognized it. I had to realize nothing I could grasp would fix anything. Somehow just one more look through my online messages may hold the answer.

It didn't matter how long I stayed glued to my computer, or how long I pined for him, my rescuer simply wasn't coming. He must be saving himself for another Cinderella and it wasn't me. I had simply been trying to find someone to take my mind off of my search for Mr. Right, and I was planning to continue until someone actually could.

We were all flawed in some way, looking for the flaws in each other we could tolerate. I was looking for someone who understood mine and saw them as quirky, or unique. Maybe then I'd feel valuable, even worthy.

I still couldn't grasp the concept that I would never find my value in any of the things, or people I had been searching for. By now, at the ripe old age of, well let's just say, somewhere over fifty, I was sure I was supposed to have learned this by now. Did I tell you I was stubborn?

I could see my guardian angel sitting on a stoop somewhere, exhausted, shaking his head, asking God, "Why me?" I'm sure my angel was begging for a reprieve. I guessed I was going to continue down this road until I learned every hard lesson I could.

"The Island of Misfit Toys allows us to imagine that maybe our flaws are actually just uniqueness misunderstood." ~ Unknown

Chapter Sixteen

~ *Add To Cart* ~

By now, I was asking myself, *what on God's green Earth am I doing?* What did I hope to accomplish? I had spent the last 31 years of my life safely guarded by a wedding ring. With a sense of security, however false, I felt protected by it. Without it, I felt like someone on an auction block.

I didn't want to auction myself off to the highest bidder. In reality, I didn't want to auction myself off to anyone at all. Here, if a guy wanted to meet me, all he had to do was click *add to cart.* I couldn't think of a more painful way to find my Mr. Right.

But, I gave in to reality once again and finally answered one of my online date requests. It would be at the very least a learning experience. So, I headed off to my first encounter with a complete stranger. I didn't know what to expect but I sat in the car until I could locate the guy I'd seen in the profile picture. One can only hope they're recognizable. That in itself was a start.

Then he appeared... a little more salt and peppered than pictured, but I didn't mind. He was charming and I was surprisingly relaxed as we shared conversation over a cup of coffee. Having both talked right through dinner, his invitation to take a walk and grab a burger was something I welcomed.

I just love a guy I can comfortably eat a burger and fries with. He actually suggested a large burger since, in his opinion, I could stand to gain a few pounds. Those words were the most romantic I had ever heard, and after them we shared a few laughs.

After another 2 hours of conversation we decided to call it a night. He was a complete gentleman. I don't know why that surprised me, but it was refreshing and I thanked him for a great evening. I knew in my heart that he was probably not the one for me, but I wasn't really looking to jump into anything this time, anyway.

It was like shopping, only with people who had feelings. I think I was interested in the process at this point because it gave me the control. I didn't want to hurt any of them any more than I wanted them to hurt me and the power to do so was in my hands.

Now I know why I wasn't a fan of the dating process. My choices could change someone's life forever and that was way too much power. When I think of the words that can build people up, there are equal numbers that can tear them down.

I have a responsibility, not only to those who cross my path, but also to myself to use them wisely. There simply weren't enough words used wisely or otherwise to soften the blow of rejection I had experienced. Since I knew the pain all too well, I certainly didn't want to deliver any of my own.

By now, I had been on two dates with online Prince #1, and actually enjoyed spending time with him. He seemed easy to talk to and I was able to be myself. He didn't expect anything and I had learned not to either.

I was pretty certain I knew exactly what I wanted in my Prince and I had a gut feeling this wasn't him. I just wanted to make it work so badly. It would eliminate the dreadful evening scroll through countless pokes, smiles and flirty messages that made me cringe. I thought if I could just make him the one, I wouldn't have to go down that road any longer. However, the glass slipper simply didn't fit.

As I walked away from our days old relationship, I felt awful yet brave at the same time. A new and fresh strength came over me. I did it! I said no! I walked away! Walking away felt good to me, however hurtful to him. It meant I had the power to choose for myself. I knew I'd rather be alone once again than be with Mr. Wrong.

I couldn't bear giving him false hope, even at the expense of loneliness. The power I carried to hurt this man was more responsibility than I wanted. I wasn't sure whether I preferred to be on the receiving end or the giving end of that equation, but for what it was worth, I kept my walls up and my heart safe from rejection on either side. I realized my heart belonged to another and the, *another,* was myself. I had finally become important enough to myself. I knew what I would and would not accept in my life.

My Prince Charming was going to be a man that shared the same love for God and ministry or He was not the prince for me. Church encompassed a majority of my time, and energy. It wasn't a place to check off a box on Sunday morning. It was the place I worshipped, the people I did life with, the parties I attended, the trips I took, the past, present and future of all I am. It's not the building but the community, the calling, and I couldn't separate myself from it. So, I was determined to move on.

My dating life was in my hands totally and that felt much better than pouring out my heart for it to be scooped up and ripped apart one more time. Boundaries were being set, only this time by me. I was feeling in control for the first time. I liked that feeling. It was the unfamiliar part of this path for sure, but one that I welcomed.

I emptied my cart and continued shopping. It became a little bit easier to respond to the next two messages. I began chatting and the thought of meeting new people and making new friends became a little more exciting. I was waiting for that moment when one of them slipped up and armor started to peek through the façade they all hid behind. I prefer the *real thing,* if you know what I mean. I'd rather know up front what I'm looking at.

Needless to say, I knew my search for Prince Charming was going to continue, albeit reluctantly. There was always an endless supply of suitors waiting to profess their undying love and devotion. Every pick-up line imaginable was displayed above each photo Cinderella chose to read, some more creative than others.

Between the *hopefuls* and the *hopeless*, there was always a very fine line. Cinderella could only hope the pick-up line was just a

117

poorly chosen window into her Prince's soul. Maybe he would redeem himself by actually being creative.

There was always the thought that a less than creative suitor might actually find me less than a perfect match as well. So, as I continued on this new and unfamiliar path, I realized that it might be lined with rejection in a completely different way. There was no way around it, under it or over it. The ground was covered in thorns and gravel but there was only one way, and that would be God's way straight through it.

I was going to go through it, whether I liked it or not, but not without His help. Of all the things I had asked God for, this certainly was not one of them. I knew it was necessary to be the woman of God He called me to be. Either way it was not going to be without pain.

Online Prince #2 was now emerging, so into the cart he went. "Wanna meet for a cocktail?" He messaged. This was not a good sign. My profile clearly stated I was a non-drinker, but I gave him the benefit of the doubt.

"I don't drink." I quickly answered back. Sometimes, days went by, before you got a response. So I waited, knowing he was probably answering several messages from Cinderella hopefuls. I don't know how they keep track of it all. Strange though, when he finally replied, "I don't either." I often wondered why he'd even asked in the first place, then.

In his only profile picture he was wearing dark sunglasses. I wasn't sure what to think about that. He was handsome from what I could tell, but the eyes reveal the soul of a person, and I couldn't help wondering what he was trying to hide. I asked for at least a peek.

"You can see my eyes when we meet," he said smugly. He appeared frustrated that I wasn't enthusiastic about meeting him. The truth is, I wasn't enthusiastic about any part of this process and I told him so.

I must have seemed a bit of a challenge, which I'm guessing he found exhilarating. "Well," he said, "I haven't seen your ankles." At least he had a sense of humor and I liked that.

"My ankles are amazing." I replied with confidence and I could sense he might be hoping I was telling the truth. If you could feel chemistry through an online chat, it was growing. He gave me his number, and asked for mine. I wasn't ready to give up the fight yet.

"I'll let you have my number when I can see your eyes," I replied. Apparently enjoying the fight as well, he responded one last time.

"I'll let you see my eyes when you give me your number."

"Touché" and with that I surrendered.

The texts came quickly, building on our recent dialogue filled with sarcasm and humor. I remember his first text. *Hi, from my eyes.* That seemed so simple yet charming enough, and I responded, *Hi, from my ankles.* I could now see, what looked to me to be a faint flicker of light, a faint hope of a fairy tale hiding in the history of an IPhone romance and we began our courtship.

Due to the holidays, we had little time to get together, so we patiently communicated through our technology. If our phones could be friends, we might stand a chance. After finishing an event with friends at a local restaurant, we finally met.

Even though I never got that picture revealing his eyes, I recognized him right away. He walked casually into the area I was sitting. He sat down next to me, unaware that a group of my closest friends were at the adjacent table ready to be entertained by the romantic comedy unfolding.

Seeing his eyes for the first time was a treat. It allowed me to drop my defenses and enjoy getting to know him. He did not, however, get to see my ankles. Laughing, I said, "Sorry, you haven't earned the right to see them yet."

When the music got so loud we could no longer hear, we decided to end our interrogation of each other. He helped me with my coat, and walked me to my car, as a Prince Charming should. I was starting to feel hopeful again. Could this be the one? I asked myself. God only knows. My heart is afraid, but I can't let it stop me from experiencing this part of the journey.

That would be our first and last date for the next three weeks. I didn't mind. I wasn't going to let my heart get involved anyway. It felt safer that way. The next two months were filled with texts, dates, even flowers. We spent time together, watching movies and enjoying each other's company, still there was something missing.

I introduced him to my friends, my family, and my church. Still, I had only been introduced to the dust and plastic sheeting covering the belongings in the home he was remodeling, no family, and no friends. I wanted to put it all out there right up front as soon as possible, but apparently he was saving me for the somewhat distant future.

I wasn't trying to rush him down the aisle, but I wanted to give him an opportunity to run as quickly as possible, if he was going to. I knew my heart might get sucked in, if I gave him too much of my time. I couldn't allow myself to let any walls break down this time.

He seemed so private, and extremely independent. I couldn't blame him. Having been single for ten years, he wasn't ready to share his life with anyone. He didn't seem to be ready to share control with anyone as well. I knew I was looking for a balanced relationship, and this wasn't it, but we got along well and I must admit, it felt good to be held again.

Something wasn't right, but I didn't want to let go of the feeling of having someone to belong to. Even though the slipper wasn't a perfect fit, he managed, if only slightly, to fill the Mr. Right shaped void. I was hoping, with just enough force, my foot would magically fit into that glass slipper. I managed, once again, to accept a less than perfect fit. *Perfect* didn't exist for me, so I felt myself settling again for Mr. *Better Than Being Alone.*

I wasn't sure if chemistry still existed with online Prince #2. I wasn't even certain what it was supposed to feel like. He was affectionate, which made me feel safe. Affection and quality time are important to me, so I was certain this relationship would at least fulfill my temporary needs. I was equally affectionate, but I was afraid it wasn't enough for the fairy tale I was searching for. I needed more, but feared it was too much to ask.

Fear will cause you to do and say things you should keep to yourself, but it can also paralyze you when you need to take action. The past was slowly coming back to haunt me. I had made a decision to be open and honest about my needs and wants, but found myself resorting to bad habits. It was easier to settle.

I was paralyzed once again as he started to pull away. It seemed like overnight the relationship vanished into thin air. I tried to keep the walls up so I wouldn't get hurt again and thank God, I did. I diplomatically and graciously let him go without a fight. As our relationship began, so it ended, and with one final text, *I wish you the best.* we parted ways.

I was confident in the way I had handled myself this time. I had come a long way since my divorce. Refusing to let my heart get involved proved to be a good decision. Friends assured me if I was *fine* after a break up, then he wasn't for me anyway. I agreed, although I shed a few tears once his final text, *'ditto'* hit my cell phone screen. Simple and to the point, but it didn't soften the sting of rejection, and that was life altering. He was simply *not* my Prince Charming.

I would rather be alone than to shackle Prince Charming to the walls of my castle. I was becoming the champion of forcing my foot into glass slippers. I truly wanted it to be right but it wasn't, and I knew it. My cart was empty once again.

In that life-altering moment, a light went off. Almost two years had gone by and it had taken me nearly all of it, a bucket load of tears, and a whole lot of prayer, to realize I may actually be destined to walk around with one missing shoe.

I was coming to grips with the fact that I may be on a *table for one* path for the duration of my life. It shattered my hopes of a Happily Even After. It never occurred to me that my fairy tale would come with a disclaimer that read: *Mr. Charming, Shining Armor and lifelong commitment 'not included'.*

I was worthy of a *Happily Even After*, even if it was in God's time and not mine. It was painful waiting on God, but it was equally painful moving ahead without Him. So, I pushed myself away from the computer determined to deal with the pain of loneliness head on.

Pain has a way of motivating us to move from one place to another. I could only hope I would find myself at a better place, with someone new and a new beginning. It would be at the end of divinely collected moments.

I knew couples that created a long history of love, and friendship through their struggles. Where would I collect that kind of history with someone now? It takes years to get to know someone like that, years I didn't have. Fairy tales don't work out for people like me. Who does it work out for any way? Ken and Barbie?

I would sit alone at the bar in my favorite local restaurant on many nights. There, the owner introduced himself, checked on me occasionally and we seemed to understand something about each other. We both experienced loss.

His name was Ken. He had lost his wife a year earlier and was still grieving. He must have seen the pain in my eyes, as I became a regular. He shared with me his story as I shared mine. I never left without taking a piece of encouragement with me. He knew what to say and I needed to hear it.

He told me their story. Her name was Barbie, Ken's wife. I giggled as I let that thought sink in. Ken and Barbie. Really? Was this a divine appointment? His face lit up with an endearing smile, yet filled with longing for his love of a lifetime. It made my heart smile to hear about such a great love.

Remembering details of their journey, and seeing the pain return to his face, I couldn't help but feel a little selfish. I had experienced loss, but the hurt was from a totally different place. It was far from unbearable. Surely letting him share helped me, but I was hoping to do the same for him. I couldn't help but think about those for whom the fairy tale works out, like Ken and Barbie. Were others that lucky?

In the movie Pretty Woman, Vivian is sitting poolside with her *soon to be* ex co-worker. She asks, "Who does it work out for, really?" Kit responds, "You mean like, you want me to give you a name?" She ponders for a few seconds as she struggles. The light comes on and you hear her shout out... "Cinderella!"

I want to believe the *Happily Ever After* story can be mine too, like Ken and Barbie, but before the wedding cake gets stale, my hopes are dashed. Where did Prince Charming go after he whisked me off to the land of unicorns and rainbows? His shining armor quickly dulled, and now gray horse was sent out to pasture. I guess I was tricked into believing the fairy tale was for girls like me.

I fell into the trap of believing it only works out for a few good people, the *perfect* couples, the *once in a lifetime* crowd, or the *one in a million* club. It's not a fairy tale reserved for Ken and Barbie, or Cinderella and Prince Charming.

It works out for those who have learned that it's a commitment of mutual respect, selfless love, and acts of will, not mere emotions. It takes two loving, sacrificial people. It doesn't work well any other way. Happily Ever After might not have been for an average girl like me, but *Happily **Even** After* was.

I wasn't the type who gave up easily. I never wanted to give up on hope. It was all I had. "Don't give up hope." Ken said, "When you least expect it, you'll find it, or it will find you." I hadn't had much luck with finding anything that resembled what I was looking for, but I hadn't lost hope either.

He was right. Maybe a silhouette would appear out of nowhere, a smile would emerge and my hopes would be renewed. He'd come out of nowhere, colors flying, flags waving, with armor polished, bright and shining. I will have met my Prince Charming and he will have come to rescue me.

"I didn't want to kiss a lot of frogs to find my Prince Charming."
Unknown

Chapter Seventeen

~ *A Damsel In Distress* ~

It was a whirlwind romance; proof that love and Happily Even After can be found in the storm and live on until the sun is shining again and the clouds have faded away into a heavenly bliss. Allen came to rescue his Cinderella, and this Cinderella, like Vivian, rescued him right back.

It was a workday, just like any other day for Allen James, nothing special, at least not yet. He was a police officer with the Jacksonville Sheriff's Office on call like any other day before. There was only one exception with this particular day. Allen had failed at marriage not once, but two times. He had been praying that God would allow him to meet HIS princess. The one who was meant for him.

He realized that if he was ever going to find his Mrs. Right, he was going to have to trust God for her and not try finding her on his own. After all, God knew him, had created him, and had certainly created and prepared a wife just for him. It was going to have to be an act of total submission and trust which would prove to be the greatest decision of Allen's life.

It was a beautiful summer day and Joie finished her work and headed to the car, to start the lonely ride home like she had every day before. This time though, she was in for a ride that would be anything but lonely. Although Joie may have seemed to most unaware men, to be frail and weak, she proved to be one strong lady that day.

With a gun pressed to her back and afraid for her life, she did what any woman would do... she followed instructions. "Get in the car", he said, as he jumped in after her. She made it clear that she would drive him anywhere he wanted to go, but she wasn't going to do anything else.

He asked for her money, and as luck would have it that day, she had only one single dollar bill to her name. As she slowed to a stop, he jumped out of the car. Apparently the single dollar was not going to get him very far, so he turned to find another victim for the day.

She went back to her office, shaken and with tears in her eyes began to relay the story to her co-workers. It was then they made the call that would change Allen's life forever.

Allen, being on call that evening, was in the downtown area. For some reason, he really didn't want to take the call that night. However, God's plan will always prevail and this Cinderella and Prince Charming will be forever grateful that it did.

As Joie sat in the back office, crying and badly shaken, her prince charming came riding up on a white horse all right. But this horse was made of metal and rubber, and had red and blue lights flashing from it.

"I knew it from the moment I laid eyes on her," Allen said. "I knew she was the one for me."

Allen, being the in charge kinda guy he was, wasn't going to waste any time making memories with his Cinderella, either. He had made note of her phone number from the police report and, in his words, "followed up" with her that night, just to make sure that she was not traumatized by the events of the day.

Within the next twenty-four hours, he drove by to see her. He remembers with a grin from ear to ear like it was yesterday. "She was wearing a cute little dress," he said, "and I remember that she had on a pair of red go-go boots."

That night he asked her to go out to dinner with him after work. She quickly agreed, and at eleven pm he took her to the place where all police officers went after the evening shift...The Pig Barbeque.

Maybe barbeque would help her find the man of her dreams? As God orchestrated their fairy tale so perfectly, they began a symphony of a lifelong love affair.

"I get paid on the first and the fifteenth, so when do you want to get married?" he asked. With no hesitation from Joie, they were married less than three weeks later.

Now, most fairy tales stop there. It was just the beginning for the two lovebirds. Time marched on and with it came moments full of ups and downs, highs and lows. They traveled together, through the maze of experiences that would either break them, or strengthen them. It's what made them who they are, and it's what will carry them through to the Happily Even After as they choose not to give up.

One night during their first vacation, while watching a live performance, one of the dancers came over and offered a kiss on the cheek to Joie's knight in shining armor. How sweet it seemed, until Allen jokingly flipped his head around to snag a kiss on the lips. Joie wasn't sure how to take that. She had never experienced anything like that before.

They had only been married a month, and just getting to know each other. He had such a great personality. She was overjoyed that her very own prince was so charming. but hadn't planned on sharing that part, or any part of him with another woman.

Marrying so quickly, she knew nothing about her new husband. For a split second, she was questioning her choice. Allen was a take-charge kind of guy, and an extrovert. Joie was very shy, and soft spoken, if she spoke at all, and was afraid to voice her opinion, at times. There weren't many disagreements, because Joie avoided confrontation. Allen didn't mind, he thought everything was fine.

In order to truly communicate in a way that would ensure a Happily Even After, counseling became necessary. It revealed a vibrant and intelligent woman inside the damsel Allen had rescued. This was something he had not seen, but he didn't want her any other way. He needed to step back and give Joie a safe place to share her heart. Both knew they had to focus on God first in order to continue this journey together.

With a new hope and trust in God, they stepped into the next chapter of their life. Allen left the police department to fulfill his life-long dream of being an airline pilot. Although Joie supported him, she knew trouble was on the way.

She felt well taken care of with the financial security of a policeman's salary, but the starting income at an airline wasn't promising. Taking this position would mean losing more than half of Allen's pay, but how much income is worth pushing aside your dream?

They pressed forward with little more than the basics, not expecting much. But, Allen was promoted within the first year, as the youngest man to ever captain this airline. That meant a raise in salary and in self-esteem. So, they quickly adjusted their lifestyle to reflect this newfound success.

There was a bit of a problem though. They weren't ready to make that kind of commitment to the debt those choices delivered, and were quickly buried underneath a load of them. With two children now, the stress became overwhelming. Joie remembers crying out to God to lead them, and help her trust Him.

"Things got pretty bad," Joie said. "We were at the end of our rope and were about to lose everything." They joined a multi-level marketing business and worked together to dig themselves out of the hole they were in. "We struggled." Joie said. "But, we weren't able to talk to anyone about it."

In the business they were in, the goal was to inspire and set an example for those who joined them. They could only share parts of their struggle or it could quickly become discouraging to those they were trying to help. "We simply couldn't share all our dirty laundry." Joie said.

"They continued their desperate attempt to rescue their family, attending meetings, events and focusing on helping others. "We loved what we did, and were to lead the way in helping others get through similar struggles." She added. "It was the best experience of our lives and we learned so much. " Joie finished. It was difficult doing the hard work together, but we had no choice.

Joie loved Allen, but certainly didn't like him at times. Love is a decision, Joie said. "We had to decide to love each other and keep moving forward anyway, in spite of our feelings," she added. "We became stronger as a result of climbing uphill together."

Joie and Allen came out of the valley with grateful hearts, each more in love with the other. The opportunity for failure was endless but they took what they were given in the valley and brought it out creating something that has now lasted their lifetime.

This kind of love, Agape love, isn't based on emotions, feelings, physical attraction, money or any earthly ability. It is a love you can only give and receive by the power of God himself. It is a love that suggests I will choose, or *will* to love you when I don't feel like it, even when you may not deserve it.

It means I will choose to act in my partner's best interest even if it hurts. It's an "I'm gonna love you, no matter what" kinda love. True love. The love that 1 Corinthians talks about, the one that "never fails". It's the only love that will carry a couple to the end of their journey through the mountains and valleys. It's a true love based on continuous, selfless acts of kindness and friendship.

"There were many times that she should have left me." Allen said with a sound of gratefulness. Joie had in return rescued her Prince Charming right back and he knew he was better off with her than without her.

"Many times we could have called it quits, but I knew if I was ever going to have the lifelong partner I had always prayed for, it was not going to be without a fight. We were both going to work for it and stick with it to the happy end." Allen said. Joie too had made a decision early on. Letting go of her own will would be required if they were to enjoy a *Happily Even After* kinda love.

"Give me what *You* want me to have, God. Make me the woman *You* want me to be for Allen." She asked. With that she let go and continues each day to trust God to mold her into His perfect design for her husband.

Selfless love is the source of happiness and fulfillment they found as they each showed continuous acts of kindness over the next 40 years, 2 children and 7 grandchildren later.

"Being a gentleman isn't about saving a damsel in distress. It's about defeating the dragon within yourself."

Unknown

Allen & Joie James

~"A happy marriage is about three things: memories of togetherness, forgiveness of mistakes and a promise to never give up on each other." ~

Unknown

Chapter Eighteen

~ *It's Complicated* ~

I can only hope when I finish my journey on this Earth, I will have left such a lasting and loving imprint on someone's life. Those I love, and those I allow to love me are all part of a beautiful story God is authoring. It was complicated. Sometimes I failed to give love or, however strange it seems, failed to receive it.

Sadly, I didn't feel worthy of it. I hid behind even my own great intentions, hoping to avoid my biggest fear, rejection. Even the thought of that awful, pain in the gut feeling caused me to retreat. I was taking a long vacation from reality with someone who didn't even like me very much, myself.

I knew it would get easier to get back in the game each time, but I didn't like playing games. It was going to make me stronger though, because it hadn't killed me yet. I was sure God wasn't finished with me. I may have turned my back on God but he hadn't turned His back on me. He had come to rescue me, over and over. It wasn't complicated to Him.

I had a broken heart, a broken home, broken dreams, and now a broken fairy tale, but God didn't mind my brokenness. He wasn't embarrassed by my mistakes, nor by me. I knew by the time this was over, I would know what it means to truly trust Him. I finally reached a milestone in my journey. I was a slow learner for sure, but I welcomed the lesson.

It's Complicated

All my relationships seemed right in the beginning. I wondered why our paths crossed in the first place if it wasn't meant to be? I wanted and needed answers once again.

"God, will you give me a sign? What am I supposed to do? Am I supposed to be alone? Am I supposed to be with someone, and if so, why had we not met yet?" I just wanted Him to un-complicate things.

I made a deal with God. *I promise to wait on You if You will give me a sign.* The Holy Spirit said, "Oh, you *will* wait, sign or not. You can worry, make your best effort, or rest in my plan, but you will wait regardless. Those were familiar words.

I had my answer. I just didn't like it. I was now in the single girls club. It seems the single girls and the ones who weren't, always wanted to swap places. I got tired of hearing ladies say how much they would prefer wearing *my* shoes. Enjoy your freedom. I'd hear, or "Girl, I wish I was single."

What was that saying about her Prince Charming? Was that fair to him? Why did they deserve to have a Mr. Right when they didn't even appreciate him? I heard even sillier things like, "You can do anything you want right now."

Really? Well, apparently not if the only thing you want to do is be with your life partner doing *life-partner* things together.

I would no longer go looking for anything. I was going to learn to like it that way, with or without my permission. It occurred to me, at this point in the journey, the smelly socks left on the floor now were mine. Dishes left in the sink were as well, and when the sounds of snoring woke me in the middle of the night, I could no longer blame anyone but me.

Now came the difficult task of changing my relationship status. Social Media was just way too nosy. Why did they want to know my relationship status anyway? After hesitating for two years, I decided it was about time for me to click that one box. Was I really single or was it truly just "complicated"?

It's Complicated

We should be limited to three relationship options: Single and Complicated, Married and Complicated or Widowed and Complicated. I was sure they were all complicated. Once I realized how little I needed or wanted *complicated,* I took a moment to re-think my plight.

The word *plight* insinuates conditions that are unfavorable, I was gonna have to find a new word to describe my, ummmm, adventure. Life is an adventure any way I looked at it. I wasn't going to give wings to negative titles any longer. So, no relationship status at all seemed more appropriate...next.

I wasn't waiting for my fairy tale to start, I was living it right here, right now, no matter how complicated it seemed. Each step I take and each choice I make is becoming part of my *Happily Even After* story, with or without my Prince.

I told myself, *this time things are gonna be different.* I had a strength I hadn't felt in years. I was free to take whichever road I chose. It has been a long time since I have acknowledged any options. I could see the whole world at my fingertips, and my fairy tale ending was yet to be completed.

Complicated or not, I could still find ways to play the victim. I could let my career; ministry and busy life keep me distracted. If I stayed busy enough, I wouldn't be held accountable for all of the things I didn't accomplish, and I was sure the enemy was afraid of my potential. I needed to find a balance, without feeling selfish.

Selfishness born from the enemy could cause me to sink inside myself, blocking out the needs of others. However, self-preservation allowed me to preserve that which God had blessed me with to be a source of encouragement and light to others through my pain. I needed to put the oxygen mask on myself first.

Every mixed up relationship I had been a part of, had many of the same elements; attraction, impatience, desire and haste but most of all, they were laced with selfishness. They all seemed to have that one common denominator. It wasn't necessarily with malice, but selfishness was in abundant supply. Where there is a giver there is usually a taker close by. Those couples that found balance were the ones living out their *Happily Even After.*

I wanted that and I would be smarter, this time. Every prior relationship, I was looking to be carried away on that silly white horse. But, with a clearer perspective I might find what I was truly searching for, true Love.

Being in a relationship for any other reason than true love, would have lowered me to a noisy gong.

> *"If I speak in the tongues of men and of angels, but have not love, I am a noisy gong or a clanging cymbal."*
>
> *1 Corinthians 13:1*

That takes *true* love. Deep down, I knew the few who had finally been awakened by true Love's kiss, were enjoying their *Happily Even After.* This kiss came in many forms, a whole new land to explore, a lifelong dream realized, or one more chance at love.

Surrendering to a sovereignty I didn't even understand, I was filled with new hope, valleys and mountains included. Alternate endings were *my* choice. When the light came on, I realized God would be okay with my imperfect future, as long as I followed Him, and all the divine appointments He placed in my path. Though, it wasn't a guarantee.

I could continue searching for Prince Charming, but what did I hope to gain by searching for a ghost? If he *was* real, my imperfection would surely infect him after joining forces. No one is perfect, no marriage is perfect and no lifetime is perfect, not even the fairy tale kind. It's in the flaws and failures we see each other through the eyes of grace. Unconditional love was the object of my search, not fairy tale feelings.

Does he make me happy? Do I feel loved? When the flutters and emotions overflowed, I decided he must be the one for me. But, that kind of affection could only fill a void. Everyone has one or more empty spaces, but true *agape* love is the only way to fill it.

God wanted me to be content, but He created someone for me to walk this journey with. He was a custom design created by God himself for my *empty* space. We would complement each other, and bring honor to the Lord for His purpose in the Earth. I didn't seem to find him, looking for him. Maybe I would by looking for True Love's kiss.

I had expected, by this season of my life to have spent at least three quarters of it with one man. The one I knew everything about and still wanted to wake up next to. *That* was the spice of life. I was afraid time was slipping away faster than I could keep up and I would have so little time with my Prince.

I wanted to enjoy a long and steady journey living out my *Happily Even After* story. I couldn't imagine spending an eternity living out a mediocre story with someone whom I shared only the space underneath the roof. To know the worst parts of someone and still want to walk this journey together was incredibly sexy.

It meant denying ourselves for the sake of each other. Denying myself doesn't come natural, but it was becoming clear that it was a necessity for a *Happily Even After*. I saw selflessness in the *lucky* couples that managed to get it right. Their fairy tale spanned a lifetime.

For the outsiders looking in, they were living a fairy tale only few experience. Not only accomplishing great things together but also adding value to each other as they added value to those blessed enough to be touched by them. **What are we willing to deny ourselves for the sake of accomplishing great things together and adding value to others?** I longed for that. I wanted to live the rest of time, no matter how short, with the one man whom I shared true love.

This next season of life will be my best ever, I thought. It will still be complicated. It won't come without struggle or trial, but it will come with a renewed sense of who I am, and a renewed faith. God allowed my pain to strengthen me, and wanted me to share it with others so they could find peace where faith meets grace.

I wasn't sure if that made me happy or afraid, but I was determined to pursue happiness in the midst of the *complicated*.

After all, I was promised life, liberty and the pursuit of it. Everyone else was searching for it too.

"I'm complicated, sentimental, lovable, honest, loyal, decent, generous, likeable, and lonely. My personality is not split; it's shredded."

Unknown

Chapter Nineteen

~ *Ladybugs Katherine, Ladybugs* ~

I wanted to be happy. So, if I found someone, anyone that made me feel happy, I guess I had arrived at my fairy tale. It came complete with a partner whom, I had imagined, was searching for the same thing. Was that really all we were looking for, happiness? Didn't we expect more from ourselves? If we didn't, why didn't we?

Happiness is fleeting and temporary. The only conclusion suggests that our fairy tale would be short lived. If we don't have the wisdom to love for more than the happiness we seek, we certainly won't live *Happily Even After.*

So this time, I was on a new mission to figure out for myself how to develop the kind of selfless love that would last a lifetime. For the sake of the commitment, I would be required to lay aside selfishness. That kind of love was possible and I knew it, but it was like a muscle that must be worked to get stronger. God established an order of things that mandates improvement with use.

The more I study, the better I'm able to comprehend. The more I exercise, the better my muscles work. The more I speak, the better I communicate. The more I love unconditionally the more love grows. I had to be stretched and challenged before I could be victorious. It didn't come easy, or without a fight.

I'm not fighting against flesh and blood, after all. I'm fighting evil in places of darkness that hate unity and love, especially the selfless, unconditional God kinda love. The enemy stands ready to keep me from becoming a powerful opponent. So, I dressed for battle, sharpened my sword and prepared for war. It's definitely worth the fight.

"For we do not wrestle against flesh and blood, but against the rulers, against the authorities, against the cosmic powers over this present darkness, against the spiritual forces of evil in the heavenly places." Ephesians 6:12 ESV

Part of me doubted, but I was hoping God was working things out for me. I was feeling a bit like Thomas, needing to see the holes in Jesus' side just to believe. I was always asking for a sign. Then it occurred to me what I was really asking for was a promise to have *my* way.

With *that* kind of promise, I would not only be patient, but I would be content in the waiting. He had already given me His promise. How many times did I need to be reminded? Romans 8:28 said that if I loved Him and was one of *the called*, He would *"work all things out for my good"*, not for my good *pleasure*, but for my good. Only He knew exactly what that meant.

Accepting mediocre relationships just for the sake of having one wasn't good for me. Even I knew that. So, why would I accept 'good pleasure' for the moment, when *good for me* lasted a lifetime? I hadn't asked to be here in the first place.

I'm not sure which land I was traveling through now, but it felt dark and lonely. I had been banished to the attic by an evil stepmother, where I found myself alone with no windows or doors, and darkness invaded every inch of the room. Light was coming from underneath the door, but I was hesitant to move towards it. I wasn't quite sure what was on the other side. I wasn't accustomed to surrendering, and with no white flag to wave, all I could do was wait for a rescuer, like a helpless victim. But, I alone could decide not to be the victim any longer. It could give me power over my circumstances.

So, I made a commitment to myself that day to wait on God's good for me. For a moment I thought about the commitment of the ink to the paper, and the permanence of a tattoo. More people were making that commitment than ever before. Tattoos were everywhere. It was proof that people could actually make lifelong commitments to something, and I joined them.

Once again like the photographs for some, the ink remained steadfast long after the fire of Love's contract had disappeared. So, my commitment to my new outlook was made and sealed in black and red and I began to walk a new path towards resting for God's best. Two tattooed ladybugs resting on my foot. It was less painful than my relationships.

That Under The Tuscan Sun Quote I couldn't get out of my mind was becoming who I was, who I wanted to be.

"Listen, when I was a little girl I used to spend hours looking for ladybugs. Finally, I'd just give up and fall asleep in the grass. When I woke up, they were crawling all over me." ~ Under The Tuscan Sun Quote

I remembered hearing this quote from my favorite chick flick many times. I could recite it from memory and I did quite often as it reminded me to stop exhausting myself with the daily search for happiness, at least the kind that came dipped in shining armor. It was the whole reason behind the tattoo in the first place.

I truly wasn't looking for a relationship. By this time I had determined I would be happy without one. Even if my resolve was short lived. I *was* surrounded by ladybugs, but I was too busy looking for them to notice them.

Sometimes I did that to myself but I had finally given up and though I never truly fell asleep, I did dose off long enough to catch a glimpse of a ladybug resting gently on my foot. It was a subtle reminder that God will provide everything I need when I decide to let go, rest, and let the ladybugs find me. And then it happened. *Ladybugs Katherine, Ladybugs*

I could see a glimmer of hope, rays of sunshine for my soul. It came in the form of a knight whose wisdom exceeded his wealth. He lifted me up out of the mud, and immediately took me away to that land I wasn't sure existed. I wanted him to fight for me, and I wasn't afraid to fight for him.

But, what would happen if after the fight, he fled to a new land? It's what I had come to fear the most. If I poured my heart into this knight, my blood sweat and tears, would it be reciprocated with the same fight for love and commitment? Was I looking for validation in my pursuit of *Happily Even After* or was I willing to just love?

What was I looking for in return for my love and sacrifice? Was a unique, and personal love in return, acceptable? I knew the failure of loves expectations, and I never wanted to abuse the privilege of another man's love. This time, I was determined to be the master of my own destiny, and I was about to get the chance to prove it. But, would I?

"Some believe that the number of spots on a ladybug's back correspond with the number of months that will pass before your wish for true love comes."

Unknown

Chapter Twenty

~ *Kind Regards* ~

This was one ladybug I didn't ask for. I was fine without one and I knew that when the right one showed up, at least I would be ready for him, this time. I could only hope that God's plan might include one beautiful, shiny suit of armor, a knight whose smile could cut through my scars and a fire-in-the-belly kind of love that would cause all others to fade in its shadow. Was this it? I asked that question several times by this point and didn't want to be disappointed once again.

We had crossed paths once before but what seemed like two old friends re-connecting, was actually a first "official" meeting. We had never even been introduced. Strangely, I felt like I had known him forever.

He reached out with a social media hello. So, I returned his "Hello Kathie" with a hello in return. Most of our virtual conversations took place at the end of long and lonely days, and were usually short and light. We certainly weren't doing things the old fashioned way, but it seemed harmless enough. This would begin the season of a gentleman's *Kind Regards* for this Cinderella Wannabe.

The conversations continued as we learned more about the moments we had each lived while in, what seemed, a whole other storybook. Similarly our stories read the same, both feeling discarded like yesterday's paper. *Finally, someone who gets it,* I thought. My heart opened enough to let a tiny bit of warmth in and it started to melt as I began to learn who this old friend was.

I could see a glimmer of armor presenting more of itself with each word he spoke. He let me in just enough to see that as my healing was coming to a close, his was just beginning. This meant that I was going to have to put my fairy tale on hold, for this knight was in no position to compete for my affections. *Here we go again, I thought to myself.*

The walls held tight. Living my life on hold was not my specialty. Patience was a virtue that I had not mastered even at this late stage in my life, not even a little. Riding a white horse into the sunset was my dream, not riding fences. If this was a *Happily Even After* scene playing out, I had been in this one before. Like the movie Ground Hog Day, repeating *some* things may be fine, but others, not so much.

I wanted to walk away but there was something beckoning me to stay. If I wanted what true unconditional love had to offer, it would be at the end of all the patience I could muster. I would be required to pack up my heart once again giving away pieces in limited doses, without the promise of any return. I seemed to be well acquainted with that proposition, and had never become fond of it.

Why was I destined to enjoy the company of knights of whom I could never boast? Why was it necessary to continue entertaining the idea of a rescuer that could not so much as wave his flag or shout my name? Because his wounds were still fresh and he was concerned for his children, there would be no relationship status updates, no pictures, and certainly no posts. That was unheard of for a hopeless romantic like me.

If you have to hide your relationship from anyone, should you even be in it? The question was a valid one for which I had and understood the answer, of course not. I couldn't be put on hold again could I? What was God's purpose for me to live in the constant *idea* of a fairy tale and not the *reality* of one? Where was the Prince Charming that came without the *sold* sign or the *sale pending* sign hanging on him? This was going to be a task and a big one if I was up for this challenge.

Kind Regards

I wasn't sure how I would accomplish it, but I knew I must, there was no question about that. It was the task of walking away in order to find love in all its glory. I wanted to rush in, at least my heart did. I wanted to wrap my emotions up in it like a warm blanket on a cold winter day. I had to let go of it for now, though in order to possess its greatness for the long haul.

A clergyman said it in a way I could grasp. He said, "If it's the real deal, you don't have to parade it around." But that was a lot to ask of me after all my heartache. "Why did God always ask so much of me?" I pondered.

I always felt I was on the brink of something great, but it always seemed just out of reach. A glimmer of hope flickered from the distance but as I inched toward it, like a mirage, it would fade out of sight. It was becoming clear to me if the fate of my *Happily Even After* was in my own hands, I would need to chase it down, clobber it and drag it kicking and screaming back home with me. But, then I'd be breaking the promise I had made to myself. I never, *ever* wanted a love that needed clobbering.

We seemed to be in agreement that living one day at a time was even too much to ask for today. Living one moment at a time might be within our reach, being honest to a fault. It was gonna hurt, but truth would always be the better option, and from what I had learned early on, it would eventually *set me free.*

We were both looking for freedom. We needed freedom from our pasts, from guilt and shame but mostly, we were interested in freedom from the fear of moving forward. We both knew there was no other choice than to move ahead. What was stopping us? What was stopping him?

Whatever it was, I wasn't interested in competing with it. There was nothing behind us but rejection anyway. He quoted the serenity prayer regularly, esp. parts he wanted so desperately to believe. *"Hardship is a pathway to peace."* It was one of his favorite quotes. He knew this and recited it over and over until eventually talking himself, at times, into believing it. We just kept waiting for the peace to arrive.

Boundary setting was a great lesson from the recent past, so I set out to put up a few of my own this time. There was sincerity in his voice and a little bit of a quiver in mine as we each moved on opposing sides of this newly set boundary. We were building together what I believed was beginning to take the shape of a foundation for a future *Us*. Was that possible? If it was, then I didn't mind this boundary so much. I knew it was necessary for any *Happily Even After.*

It didn't take long for us to break our own rules. We were like magnets, drawn to each other. Hurting souls find other hurting souls to listen, if only to the sound of the other breathing, or to feel the rhythm of a broken heart beating. I found healing there. I thought healing could be shared, but there is only so much you can do. A man must find his own way. I could support and encourage, but couldn't administer healing. If *timing is everything* then everything was bad. If timing was a virtue, I hadn't mastered it any more than I had patience. They were inseparable.

We may have had bad timing, or maybe it was just the wrong time altogether. Still, we fed such a hungry part of each other that time didn't seem to matter anymore at all. We dared to support each other with the best of what we had left to offer. Time didn't possess enough clicks on a clock to end the healing dialogue we shared. We could hear the sound of each other's heartache, and like a salve, made the wounds feel better.

I felt a kinship with his sorrow, and knew he felt one with mine. With our circumstances, and the honest promises we made to stay on our own side of the fence, we had a fight on our hands. It left the door open for intruders. We agreed we were in this together. I didn't want someone shouting encouragement from outside the ring. I wanted someone in my corner. I felt it was the only way to protect what we were building.

If my Prince Charming didn't think our fairy tale needed protecting, his perspective needed an adjustment. If he didn't want to defend our fortress, I guess I would need to grab another sword. All I know is that I never wanted to feel afraid again. But, that was one wish even a fairy godmother could not grant.

I was going to learn to fight afraid, love afraid, and live *Happily Even After* afraid, or find the courage to conquer fear itself. To *not* fight, *not* love or *not* live, was not an option. Fear was the enemy and I was preparing for its funeral, with or without Mr. Kind Regards.

We were both fighting, but *his* fight was within. He cared to look within and see all the ugly. It took a lot of courage to see himself from the view of someone else. I knew if he cared enough to ask the hard questions, he was on his way to healing.

I wanted us to be people who could admit we are capable of utter failure, people who were honest enough to admit our own insufficiency. It would allow us to offer much more grace to one another. He was willing. I was willing, and that was a start. Was it enough to hang onto? Should I stay on this path or take a detour?

I wasn't sure which direction would take me to the greatness I had hoped for, but taking God's road was the plan for now. Its' shoulders were lined with the most hope. His way was the road less traveled. It could possibly be the loneliest, but He was my friend and stuck by me. He held my hand at times and carried me at others, but He never left my side. He reminded me that the end of this journey was not where the joy was found, but in the journey itself.

I was actually right in the midst of my *Happily Even After* whether I was on the mountain or in the valley. The view was just as beautiful either way. From the valley, I could see the mountain, and from the mountain, I could see the world.

Happily Even After was here and now, and I believed this prince wanted to join me in the journey. His armor was worn and his face carried the pain of his past. He had earned every wrinkle and scar being the man that God designed him to be. They were endearing and charming, each telling a unique story of victory.

He was a strong soul with a gentle spirit, engulfing me in tenderness. A passion for good flowed out from him and covered every part of the unfamiliar path he was forging for himself. He was a true knight with his sword drawn. He wanted to fight against all the weapons the enemy could throw, but was he willing to fight for me?

Though this was a journey he did not choose, he was willing to take it. We were both grieving a great loss, and prayed that our suffering would not be in vain. It was bonding us together like no earthly glue could, I thought. I quickly discovered that he was not capable of a bonding of any kind, for now, and I would have to agree with myself that I was okay with that.

Because his heart still belonged to someone else, it was going to take time, and time was slipping away. I couldn't fight for a knight whose heart was intent on rescuing a dead dragon. It was painful to watch, from my side of the fence, as he wielded his sword in every direction, without victory.

So, I determined, as if determination was a marriage all to itself, to keep boundaries in place and be true to my beliefs. It wouldn't be easy. After all, I'm only human. Together, we wanted to win this war, and conquer our doubts, fears and human frailty. Maybe it was just for a season, but it would take on a personality all its own as our souls longed to stay connected even when our physical bodies couldn't. I secretly longed for the day when worry, doubt and fear would be replaced by a warm hug that said *we did it.*

Although I was the kind of girl who didn't give up easily, I wasn't sure how much fight I had left in me. Stubborn was my middle name, and I wanted to fight for my *Happily Even After*, especially if I had someone fighting with me for it instead of against me.

I knew this prince was different, but there would be times that remnants of our unpacked baggage would find themselves sneaking out. Instead of stuffing them back in the bag, or hiding them under the carpet, they found the courage to expose themselves. I was hoping the remnants would be turned into shreds of hope for a new set of clean and empty luggage. It wouldn't happen overnight, and the enemy was always reminding me of it as it came pouring out once again. Insecurity...

Insecurity was my enemy and I feared it would once again get the better of me. I needed him to understand, he had to join me in slaying this dragon rather than lay his weapon down in surrender. It was the only way I could truly believe my heart was safe as I waited. I wasn't going to wait on my side of the fence any other way. It was who I had become, and who I would now forever be.

So what if my number one need was reassurance? What if my flaw was that I needed to be reminded I was loved and wanted, was that so fatal? Was it wrong? We each had something from our past that gnawed on us. My bruises were fading, but it would take him leaving his past behind before his would begin to heal. I didn't know if he had the faith or the will to do it.

I felt as if I was always on the brink of something good, but could never take hold of it. I could see the gap closing on this relationship, but I felt in my spirit it was meant to be. I think it was unconditional love I was experiencing for the first time. I not only wanted to receive it, I wanted to give it. I thought I had been there before, but was let down.

This time I was looking for it in different ways and much more closely. He rose to the challenge and with every comforting word, and every response, reassurance came. He proved my need was not invalid, or ridiculous. That's when we began to unpack and it felt great.

We lived life doing simple things, the kind of things that tend to fade with familiarity. If that was the case, I never wanted to get too familiar. We did things that couples do together to bring joy to each other's lives. With a mutual respect and understanding, we *got* each other. It was as if we were an old married couple, but just friends. There didn't seem to be any less commitment or loyalty than if we had been married. We both actually knew how to do *married* well.

Then everything changed. Well maybe not everything, but the blow was enough to leave a mark. During a deep conversation, his words revealed to me that his heart was not mine to care for. His healing was slower than expected. He was not ready to move forward, even taking a step backward at times. I couldn't do it for him, no one could.

Kind Regards

Back to my side of the fence I went. There was a connection building that made us both uneasy. It was for the best we told each other and tried talking ourselves into believing it, but it didn't make it any easier. I knew he wasn't responsible for my happiness, but being with him made me happy and being without him made me sad.

He couldn't promise me tomorrow any more than I could promise him even today. We would take it one day at a time, as usual. We had no choice, but if I *did* wake up tomorrow, being with him would still make me happy and being without him would still make me sad. Those were promises I *could* keep.

I have loved this man my whole life, or at least the idea of him. It was becoming clearer to me as the layers started to peel away. He was the Prince Charming I dreamed of as a little girl, at least from what I could see from my side of the fence. Certainly not perfect, but he seemed perfect for me. Flawed and scarred clearly, but forgiving, kind, loving and honest, painfully so at times.

He presented himself with only one assurance; "There's no greatness in me." He offered. Humbled and broken, he was incapable of presenting anyone, but the bruised and scarred man that stood before me. It was actually refreshing. The world was full of greatness already, mostly self-proclaimed, so I was okay with goodness instead. His goodness gently forced its way out of his every gesture, every word.

Time came when parts of the fence came down and the boundary lines faded a bit. We clung to the future version of ourselves. I never want to lose the wonder of that moment our eyes first met, our lips first touched and I felt the universe rearrange itself to accommodate such an extraordinary love. No matter how extraordinary, it was still a choice for me to make in the long run.

Happily Even After required a love that suggests I will choose, determine, or will to love you when I don't feel like it or when you may not deserve it. It means I will choose to act in your best interest even if it hurts. It's an *I'm gonna love you no matter what* kinda love, true love. The love that 1 Corinthians talks about, a love that never fails. It's the only love that will carry a couple to the end of their journey through all the mountains and valleys they may cross. It's a true love based on continuous selfless acts of kindness and friendship.

I was beginning to feel that kind of love for Mr. Kind Regards. I couldn't help myself. I tried to talk myself out of it with the same reasoning I had in the past. Refusing to let myself get caught up in another *not so fairy tale* relationship again, I tried to add an extra lock to the gate around my heart. I told myself he wasn't the only one for me. He wasn't going to distract me from my new, *to my own self be true* outlook on life.

I was gonna be stronger this time. I promised to be faithful to God and myself and never let another soul take a piece of my heart. I don't care how many times I repeated this new code to myself, this time it was different. I think it's because I *did* believe he was the one for me.

I knew it would distract me from my new *self first* attitude. There can only be so much *self* in a covenant. I was stronger this time and I was going to remain faithful to God. I knew this time the man with whom I shared this kind of love would help me stay there. He would be seeking the same in me.

For the first time in my life it all made sense. He wasn't the perfect Prince Charming and that was okay. He didn't always carry a sword and that was okay too. He didn't distract me from my new outlook. He encouraged it. I *was* stronger this time. Being faithful to God didn't need to be forced, and he wasn't taking anything at all from my heart but adding to it.

I was changed. I wasn't the same girl now that I was when all this began. My heart went freely this time without fear for I felt my heart knew it was safe with him. I knew one day someone would come along and love me without letting me become irrelevant. I asked again, "was he the guy?"

I wasn't sure he would ever want to be. My many personalities would introduce themselves over time. If any one of them were dismissed or frightened away, I would collect them all and walk away. Instead, as each one emerged, they were welcomed and encouraged to express themselves fully. They were received and loved for the strengths and weaknesses each one possessed, knowing together they made up this complete person.

An awakening happened for me as one after the other felt safe enough to be unveiled. Intrigued a bit by each one, he found them oddly manageable and quirky. In fun, he began naming each one. It gave them freedom to express themselves. I say this with all joking aside. Women have multifaceted personalities and only strong men, secure and honorable men, can free them all to be part of the woman they love. He did that for me. I will never forget it.

Days turned into weeks, months, and all the while our challenge, for now, was taking moments at a time. With that mindset, we were able to freely spend time together learning more about each other. Our first Holiday together was quiet and simple and as the whole world celebrated, we started the countdown.

"I've been looking for you
since my first fairy tale."
Unknown

Chapter Twenty One

~ *Countdown To A New Year* ~

The sun was beginning to set as fast as the temperature was dropping. Even to those accustomed to temperatures in the 50's, it was a chilly and blustery day. To this Florida girl, it was just plain cold.

Mr. Kind Regards and I were together to celebrate a new season in our lives. It was New Year's Eve. To us, it had lost its luster, but we were determined to rectify that. I was looking forward to this holiday with a desire to create new memories for both of us. Days that originally brought us so much happiness and joy, now brought only tears and sorrow as our memories died like spent fireworks.

It wasn't filled with the usual friends, family members or party items. There were no hats, horns or confetti, just two people with the same desire to say goodbye to the old and reach out to receive the new, whatever that might mean.

We shared thoughts about our own failures, what personal roles we played in our life story, and our hopes for what might lie ahead. Being careful to keep them realistic, we kept walls up as scorned people do. We learned, by now the hard way that the Happily Ever After was always *Happily **Even** After* in disguise.

There was nothing real about *ever* happy or *ever* after. It was all a fairy tale. Not even the, so named, battery was *ever* ready. It needed to be recharged to be productive. There was nothing that said we would be happy. It truly was a choice each one of us would have to make.

We chose to spend this season together figuring it all out. Surely we both wanted to try this thing one more time, but I couldn't help hearing Yoda in the back of my mind saying, *"Try not. Do or do not. There is no try."* It had become my mantra.

If love was a decision, a choice, then certainly two people could make the same choice to work at loving each other together, at the same time and actually *do, not just try.*

We watched as one lucky couple made that decision. They were embarking on a new journey that would begin right in front of us as we witnessed from our beachfront balcony that cold night.

Huddled up and sharing a blanket, we listened to the sounds of laughter flying through the air. Girls giggling with a familiar naivety caught my attention. I supposed God was painting a picture right there in the sand.

Oh, the irony of it all, I thought. I remembered the wedding I had seen a couple years before on this very same beach. After all I had been through, I felt like a totally different person watching this time.

The cynicism had faded along with my bitterness and I was finding a peace I had long forgotten. Even with the temperature dropping and hair doos flopping, nothing could stop this union from taking place.

The photographer was conducting the orchestra of events for the moment, marking spots on the man-made patch of green just above the bulkhead. He was carefully placing each lady so purposefully around the beautiful, yet shivering bride. He was making adjustments for their long, windblown strands of hair.

If there were bridesmaid's dresses fit for this kind of cold, they were neglected by this celebration. I couldn't help but wonder how those girls with their strapless dresses were going to make it to the end of this wedding.

That very moment it occurred to me, we put so much effort into our weddings. We fight for just the right venue and just the right dress. We fight through the details just to make this one very special moment the most memorable one of our lives. We compromise on the guest list, the reception, even the cake. We compromise when letting our crazy aunt sing her *slightly pitchy* version of The Lord's Prayer. We even fight family members on the choices we make in our mate. We fight through all of the elements and adversities to get the deed done.

But, what happens down the road when things go wrong, when things aren't just right? Did we forget how to fight through the elements? Did we forget we were in this together? We had just spent all of our parent's money. Our piggy banks were empty. We had dominated our friend's schedules and even said we wouldn't forget we were a team, *Us*.

We stood hand in hand making promises to fight against any foe, together. What happens to us, or in us that takes away the spirit of conation, that burning in the belly, instinctive drive to fight for what we want so desperately? Did we just stop wanting it?

Don't misunderstand. No one should stay in abusive or dangerous situations, **ever,** without getting help. But why was that even an alternative to the unions God had placed before us? Why were so many people having to make that choice to begin with? The enemy knew the answer to that question. He was keeping it to himself, though. I knew it had something to do with pride, and a whole lot of deep, hidden pain.

I had been there twice before and I didn't understand it myself. Things got out of control and I was left to pick up the pieces and start over. Thankfully, God was the God of second chances. I knew, though I didn't deserve it, He was also the God of third and fourth chances too. All I needed was one more chance and hoped this was the beginning of it. One cliché I didn't mind now was, *Third time's a charm,* and I was hoping to prove it right.

We watched intently as each of the characters entered the scene one by one. Everyone involved had made a pledge, or at least signed a contract, to see this happy couple seal their vows.

The van carrying familiar white folding chairs arrived just in time, and two men placed them safely in front of the decorative arbor being anchored in the soft beach sand. It seemed to be swaying in the cold trying to make its escape in the blustering winds. As for lighting the ambient flambeaus, there was even someone responsible for that.

Keeping the flame lit on the torches, with this kind of wind seemed ironically important to this whole scenario. Since the sun was setting quickly, it was the only light and warmth to be found. If gray was a feeling, it felt as gray as it looked. I'm positive there was a hotel or rental nearby where grandmas, aunts and others were seeking refuge.

In just a few short moments, guests would fill the cold seats on this empty beach. They would find sand in their shoes, salt in their hair and spray from the surf on their lips. But nothing could stop the warmth and light from pressing through what seemed to be a dreary blanket overhead. These two intent hearts shared a burning desire to see their union sealed forever.

Gray was now being replaced by black as the sun slipped behind the horizon. The moon and the flame from the torches provided the only remaining light. As guests arrived and were seated, the attendants came forward and the clock sped up. Funny, how the temperature can lengthen one's stride.

Coincidentally, the bride and groom would now have *pep in their step* and they would be husband and wife as quick as one could say *I Do*. We heard shouts of, *Let's roll, Get er dun*, and *Let's do this,* flying into the air, with a sense of impatience. After all, the vows had been pre-written. The exchange of rings was a no-brainer as well. It was a ritual most had recited at some point as a young and hopeful.

Certainly there was nothing out of the ordinary. It was just another wedding. The wedding isn't the important part anyway, the marriage is. Happily Even After doesn't rely on a perfect wedding. It didn't rely on her vow. It didn't rely on his. It was more about the *Us* they were creating, which included God. He was the only one that could make *Us* out of a man and a woman.

Both partners had to be equally committed to God and to each other to experience it. I wondered whether this couple would be one of the blessed ones. They had the capability.

I quietly bowed my head and begged God to cover them in His presence and if they didn't know Him, they would be drawn to Him. In their seeking, maybe they would find the glue I had been talking about.

I didn't have enough glue in myself. I didn't even have the means to produce it. I wasn't capable of the type of love required to hold a marriage together. That love could only be found in God. He is the glue.

As the torches were snuffed out and the party exited the beach to a warmer venue for celebrating, we continued the New Year's Eve celebration of our own. We had invited his sister and brother-in-law to share in this part of our journey, family to stand in agreement with us.

We welcomed their affirmation at our attempt for a new tradition and they seemed more than happy to give their stamp of approval. They didn't know it but having them join us for our own hand prepared meal, was secondary to enjoying the encouragement they were bringing to the table.

They were a couple with their own story to tell and I was personally grateful to have them tell it. They were in the minority, those who had lived it, struggled through it and kept their torches lit. They had found the glue. I watched them, I listened and I hoped this new chapter in our life could somehow encourage others as they had us.

Story after story kept laughter at the table for hours. It was a breath of fresh air and I longed to be worthy of the future I finally believed I could possess. They must have sensed our desire to spend those famous last 10 seconds of the year alone and I was looking forward to it. I felt acceptance as they said their goodbyes. It was something I needed and would never ask for myself.

I was hoping that a brand new chapter would come at the stroke of midnight. Like Cinderella rushing back to fulfill her promise to her fairy Godmother, I was anxious for the countdown to a new chapter in this new life I had never imagined.

I felt as if I would find my home in his embrace and that it might be the cure for my loneliness. I wasn't really lonely, but I wasn't supposed to be alone. I knew that. I felt it in the deepest part of me and knew that God had designed my prince to feel that same longing.

We each had options. We both had God, family, friends, work and hobbies. Seemed like life was complete. But, we both also had a longing for an ideal that was set in our hearts from an early age.

I knew there had to be *one* man who had my name on his heart. He was yet to be found though I had tried many times before. This time seemed different. He knew me. He saw me. He saw through me and still there was a connection none could deny.

Then it came. There was no ball to drop this year and we didn't mind. It seemed appropriate that as we were agreeing to change our own traditions for good, an icon for New Year's Eve was no longer with us. Dick Clark may have been watching from heaven, but the iconic ball wasn't signaling the countdown. Things would never be the same and yet the world would still move forward into the unknown to celebrate what was to be.

We were no different. Our story would be the same, even if it killed us. We *would* move forward and although I wanted to run, he would be much safer with a leisurely stroll. He wasn't going anywhere fast and this would test my fortitude in the months following. Whether he wanted it to or not, time wasn't going to stand still at his command, so we welcomed the New Year and celebrated what was *right now*.

The whole world was celebrating with us. At least it looked that way from our 7th floor panoramic view. Fireworks were abundant from every angle and with each sparkling explosion our resolve grew. Our resolve to do, not try. So, with a ten, nine, eight and counting down to one, we shouted the numbers out together.

Happy New Year! With a hug I wished would last forever, we said to each other. *"One day at a time."* That's all we had and that's

158

all we were able to give. I couldn't think of anyone I'd rather take one day at a time with more. We would develop a beautiful friendship without expectations. This was certainly unfamiliar to me.

It would require a whole lot of patience and trust. I was sure I had never mastered either of these virtues. There was no better way to find out exactly what I was made of than being required to follow through on my promise to trust God. I started to believe taking one day at a time was just another way of saying we were both too afraid to move forward, but neither of us had a choice.

Before he left that night, we made a promise to live our *one day at a time* journey with openness and honesty, helping each other wade through the mire of our past lives. It was the only way to live anyway, but we knew there was some heavy baggage to carefully unpack if we wanted a long and healthy relationship. He said I had no past and called himself *WYSIWYG* (what you see is what you get). I knew what he meant. He seemed to get it.

We made a relationship out of getting each other, being ourselves and filling voids that drowned out the voice of rejection. Was it true love or just companionship? He might love the idea or the feeling, but could he love me? Could he love me *enough*? *I have loved that way before and I believe I will again, someday.* He would say. I didn't find much comfort or reassurance in his honest response.

I said I loved honesty, and he was always willing to deliver it. I knew it was going to be difficult, but I thought I could love us enough for both of us. It would be healing I said, but who was I kidding? I had tried that on more than one occasion and got the same results.

"Insanity is doing the same things over and over and expecting different results." ~ Albert Einstein

So I guess if he was correct, then I must be a bit insane. Was there a cure for that? If there was, maybe it was *change*. I needed change but the older I got, the harder that became. We agreed with statements like; this is the way God made me. Love me for who I am. Love me at my worst or you don't deserve me at my best.

We agreed because true love is unconditional. However, I knew God never intended us to stay the way we are. God's unconditional love should motivate us to pursue righteousness just as our partner's unconditional love should motivate us to grow into someone more lovable, not just tolerable.

True love sacrifices so I stayed the course. We had life to live, a journey to walk. His honey-do list was a mile long as was his endless load of un-ironed dress shirts and neither of us seemed to mind. "You give me purpose." He said, and I loved that because giving him purpose seemed to give me mine.

Every time I looked into his eyes I saw forever there. As he held my hand in his it felt like home. Although I was able to keep walls around my mind, it wasn't so easy for the ones around my heart. With every act of love, one more piece of stone fell away. I was falling again though I had determined not to and one day at a time I was becoming more and more vulnerable.

"He who cares the least holds the most power." ~ Unknown

This was a revelation of the worst kind. I never wanted to be in that position again. I always seemed to be the one with the least power in any relationship. I tried not to care so much but it's who I am. I didn't know how **not** to and I watched helplessly as all the power drained out of me.

"The more you care, the more the world finds ways to hurt you for it." ~ Jupiter Ascending movie

The world already found enough ways to do that so I prayed its vendetta against me would end.

Months later, and feeling almost completely out of power, I took a step back once again. I began to realize I not only wanted, but also needed power back. I remembered my promise to myself that I would never fall so far again, and in one conversation my world turned upside down. It needed to be upside down in order for it to be turned right side up for good.

My desire was to unpack our baggage together, but there was one piece so full and bound up so tightly that only a miracle could open it. Once opened, even then, it would take great struggle to unpack it. I wasn't capable of helping, but I knew the one who was, and He was ready and waiting for the invitation. There was only one problem. I was in the way.

Getting out of the way was going to be one of the toughest decisions I have ever made. This baggage wasn't foreign to me, but it was completely foreign to him. Even still, he needed to unpack this one alone.

It was the idea of starting over, adjusting an ideal made of stone, and accepting defeat without feeling like half of a soul. I'd been there, done that, and the t-shirt had been worn, but those lessons were for me. He had to experience his own.

Walking away from *love* for the benefit of another is not a concept I grasped easily. But to truly love someone, you must be willing to sacrifice, even if it hurts you... even if it hurts them. I guess at that moment I was agreeing with God for the first time instead of fighting him. So I grabbed a box of Kleenex and headed for that lonely chair in the corner of my room again, but this time on my knees.

Mr. Kind Regards would need to make some tough decisions and I was silently rooting for his success. I knew there was no *Happily Even After* on our current path. There were too many unknown twists and turns. He would need to go to his corner and I to mine. When we came out of the corner and up from our knees we would be unstoppable, healed and whole, ready to fight for love together. At least that's what I hoped for. There was no telling how long that might take.

Sadness rushed in. Worry, doubt and fear weren't far behind. Memories came flooding in and with every song, sight, smell, and sound, I found him there. My eyes opened in the morning and the silence there in my room said no *'good morning'* was coming. Busying myself during the day was my only refuge. Each night as I lay beside tear soaked tissues, the enemy reminded me I wasn't worth loving, not even worth the fight.

"There once was a hole in the middle of the sea..." Mr. Kind Regards would begin. Now all I could think of was, there's just a hole in the middle of me. The battle for my thoughts raged on until I finally drifted off to sleep clutching my tear-stained pillow. My eyes could no longer wait for a *'good night'* that would never come.

It's for the best; I told myself and fought to actually believe it. I knew what *best* for me was. How could this be best for anyone? There was love, and acceptance on one side, rejection on the other. Freedom and forgiveness were on one side, condemnation and un-forgiveness on the other. It seemed like a no-brainer to me, and many of those watching from the sidelines, but it wasn't so easy for him.

Lifelong covenants between God and man aren't so easily broken and I understood. It's what I had longed for my whole adult life. It was a quality I found refreshing and completely annoying at the same time.

It's what I prayed for. "God, please bring someone into my life who believes in commitment, someone who believes in forever!" I begged. God *does* answer prayer, and He answered mine, just not quite like I had imagined.

My prince *was* that guy. I just didn't realize his commitment to forever would include an ideal that didn't include me. He was nowhere near ready, although he might have wanted to be at times. He could never reconcile it with his own heart. It was honorable, however unrealistic. Unrealistic for him or not, it was my reality, and my *Happily Even After* lay in the balance. How did I make this choice again?

I guess the Land of Realistic Expectations was now my permanent home, but it felt like the Land of Oz. If I just kept following that stupid yellow brick road I might find a brain, a heart, some courage and my *real* home. But I could see the Emerald City from here, why couldn't he?

I told myself that the yellow brick road was where I would be able to think, feel and be brave enough to reach the city that could show me the way home, so I didn't want to miss the journey.

However, the story reminded me that home was right there all along. If I could just click my heels together, like Dorothy, I might wake up and find all that I loved surrounding me. I just couldn't seem to wake up.

If there ever was a man who possessed honor, loyalty and strength of conviction, it was Mr. Kind Regards. He was absolutely perfect, exactly what I had asked God for. He was the epitome of the word covenant. I knew if I possessed a fraction of the patience he had in loyalty, I'd be safe with him. It felt right.

I certainly wanted to wait for the right relationship. When it's *right*, it's alive and active, altering each partner for the better. A relationship is a ministry, a testimony to the world starting with your family and friends. It's not a one-time event that creates a union of happiness. It's a million tiny events that create a union of Godliness. I could see the potential, why couldn't he?

I was going to spend the next chapter of my life watching a million tiny events take place with Mr. Kind Regards. I wasn't sure if a union would ever be created out of it. Godly or not, but I was praying I would find contentment.

I had God's promise. If He was sovereign, what right did I have to question His authority? Who was I to plead with God to change His divine will for me? I had held onto my own hopes and dreams, my own ideals and plans for so long, I didn't know how to let go, but I could think of no greater way to be content.

"Here, before Your alter, I am letting go of all I've held, of every motive, every burden, everything that's of myself..."

Kari Jobe

It's only in letting go of all I've held onto, that I can truly be content. Letting go of Mr. Kind Regards was always simple, never easy. I wanted to believe this was my fairy tale. Like Meg Ryan in the movie, *You've Got Mail,* I so wanted it to be him. My love for him was strong enough, wasn't it? I didn't have 68 years left to prove it, like Jackie, but I did have today.

"It's only possible to love Happily Even After on a daily basis."

Unknown

Chapter Twenty Two

~ *Not Even A Dog Fight* ~

68 Years is a long time together to prove your love for each other. I'm sure there were more than a million tiny events that altered not only Jackie and Julian but also, the people around them who were honored to know them.

Jackie has been a faithful salon client for over 20 years. Due to a decline in her mobility, I was now going to her home every two weeks for hair services. At times we talked about my love life, or the lack of one. She always had good advice and encouraging words. It was a safe place to share my pain.

She talked fondly of her family, especially the love of her life, showing me pictures filled with smiles. It was quiet now, but the laughter could still be felt through the walls of this home where she had spent so many years nurturing them.

She, and her husband Julian had spent so many years making memories in this very room. Her kitchen was still packed with the everyday memorabilia that made a recipe for *Happily Even After*, and she loved sharing her recipes.

Jackie rarely mentioned anything that didn't relate back to the great times she spent with family and friends here. I felt so honored to be a part of some of the sweeter moments. A smile always shined through the pain of her loss due to the great love she was blessed to share.

"Better to have loved and lost, than to never have loved." She reminded me of this quote regularly as she listened to my on-again, off-again, relationship dilemmas. She seemed to be in as much pain hearing about them as I did revealing them. I preferred listening to her story. It gave me faith in what tomorrow could bring.

Julian Armand McKenzie, Jr. was born on April 8, 1924 during the Calvin Coolidge years, as Disney created his first cartoon, "Alice In Wonderland". He was a strapping young man with high hopes and a whole lot of energy. He was everything you would ever hope your son would be, including captain of the football and track teams, Most Popular, Best All Around, President of the student body and not lacking for friends.

It was 1946. He was a lifeguard and had recently been discharged as ensign from the U.S. Navy where he served as a Naval Communications Officer.   He apparently had communications skills. However, Julian had a little bit of a disadvantage in the dating game as he had a habit of wearing cut off shorts with no shirt, sporting lots of facial hair and chewing a mouthful of tobacco. He certainly wasn't going to get a date with Jackie that way.

Jackie was born Jacqueline Newsom on June 28, 1928 as the first Air Conditioned office building was opened in the United States. She was a student at Coker College. She knew she would one day find her Prince Charming but never imagined that it would be the story she now tells.

In 1947, coincidently as *Sweethearts* opens in New York, Jackie and Julian's hearts will arrive at that one moment in time we all hope for. It was the meeting of their hearts that was destiny in the making. Julian's heart just forgot to tell his face, and it would appear that he, in order to convince Jackie, would need to visit not only a barbershop but a clothier as well. He would however, battle with giving up the chewing tobacco throughout their life together.

Being a lifeguard, Julian had more interested ladies than most, but he had his eyes fixed on a natural beauty he saw on the beach one day. She was always with "some other guy" Julian remembered. But she was absolutely gorgeous and he was, if nothing else, going to tell her so. So he did.

"He told me my longs legs were what attracted him." Jackie said. She stood tall with her shoulders square. It was a quality he admired. Most of the other girls, he knew always slouched, with little confidence, which he found unattractive.

He walked up to her with all the confidence of a gorilla, and from what Jackie says, could have passed for one at the local zoo. He was a very handsome man somewhere under all that hair, but it wouldn't be revealed until later.

"Will you go with me to the Johnny Long Dance at the Ocean Forest Hotel?" He asked. Now I'm sure his confidence was high, but only for a split second as Jackie replied. "I wouldn't go with you to a dog fight." That was the end of it for her, or so she thought.

They never made it to the dance that night, and some guys would have given up, but not Julian. He wasn't accustomed to not accomplishing his goals or winning the girl of his dreams. So as destiny would have it, he did what any good Prince Charming would do. That's right, he visited the barber, dressed in his best attire, spit out the tobacco, at least this once, and saddled up for a ride on his white horse setting out to win the heart of his Cinderella. This time Jackie wouldn't be able to resist.

She continued to go out with other guys, but Julian continued to put his name in the hat, and never gave up trying. He was the funniest guy she had ever met, and she enjoyed his company. They went to a few movies together and then it happened.

Almost overnight, he became the most handsome and funny man she had ever met. Jackie taught her children, *when you meet the man/woman you'll marry you'll just know it. It will be almost immediate.* "Look for nice lips and a nice butt." Jackie added, as she giggled. She was swept away.

It didn't take Julian long to pop the question, because he too had found exactly what he was looking for and didn't want her to get away. She was 3 months shy of her 20th birthday and her mother was a little nervous about her being so young but Julian's charm apparently worked on her quickly as well. Jackie remembers that her father, while impressed with her new fiancé, said, "I loved her first, but I approve."

They spent most days enjoying their family and friends. Both being night owls, they hosted many parties at their home until the wee hours of the morning. It seems like they had it all together. When I asked Jackie if she and Julian had faced any tragic events in their life or at least life altering ones. She responded with giggles, "Well having 3 children was life altering."

Jackie and Julian had three children, Steve, Ann and Laura who are all still happily married today. They were brought up the same way where divorce was never the solution. A woman of faith, Jackie's mom passed on a great legacy of love and commitment along with a great sense of family. They have 5 grandchildren, 4 step-grandchildren, and 1 great granddaughter.

"We just never thought of divorcing." Jackie said. "In those days it just wasn't even an option. It wasn't something either of us ever considered." As a matter of fact, no one in Jackie's, or Julian's family before them had ever divorced. "It wasn't always perfect but it was wonderful and has never been dull." She said.

Julian found out the hard way that Jackie was not the type of woman to put up with much monkey business anyway. As a matter of fact, on one occasion, Julian came home to an empty house. Jackie had relocated to the corner hotel for the evening when her prince charming failed to return home at an appropriate hour. "I just left", she said. "He decided to spend the evening with co-workers and didn't think it was important to let me know. He never made that mistake again, though."

Jackie claims there were just a lot of good times and the normal amount of real life experiences that made their life nothing out of the ordinary. She attributes their success to the great mutual respect they shared for each other. But everyone who knows their story knows they were no strangers to trials. You don't stay married for 58 years without them, even in a Cinderella story like theirs.

In June of 1998, Jackie and Julian were celebrated for their beautiful marriage of fifty years. Family and friends honored them with a weekend of laughing, dancing and sharing stories of how they met and fell in love. There was never a mention of any struggle, though I knew very well, and so did everyone else, there had to be plenty.

I wondered if they were so successful because they never dwelled on any of it. They never brought any of it to memory, and only seemed to focus on the half of the glass that was full. Even when I asked for a story to write there was nothing. Jackie couldn't stir any negativity at all. Whatever could have been remembered simply wasn't. Jackie said. "We just lived for the good times."

"For I will forgive their wickedness and will remember their sins no more." Hebrews 8:12

I don't think it's because God has a bad memory, but because he *chooses* not to remember. Jackie and Julian followed this principle. They chose not to remember the struggle, and it proved to be the best thing they could do for their family.

Steve, their oldest said, "Love, it just happens. It's a gift from God, and it happens in the strangest places and in the most unusual circumstances." He knew this all too well, asking his wife to marry him in the Raleigh-Durham airport. "You balance it all out." He continued, "You take the good with the bad and you try to settle for the in-between." He has been married to his wife, Gail, for over 30 years. Gail smiles as she talks about love letters Steve won her with, and attributes their personal success to great, and gracious role models.

Ann, their middle child who shares her dad's humor, said she always felt loved and appreciated. It was a happy childhood. Mom always taught me to stand up straight. "Apparently, that is attractive to some gentlemen." She shared.

She remembers her dad, coming in her bedroom at night with his, 'five feet long hands', brushing the hidden cracker crumbs from under her covers, to tuck her in, and wish her a good night. "I was blessed to have this family." She finished.

Laura, her youngest, and one most resembling her mom said, their tenacity and love for each other was inspiring. "There was never a doubt, they loved people, their children, and were always interested in their community." Laura remembers. Jackie was always stylish and funny, and Julian was one of the funniest people she had ever known. Together they were described by their youngest as *the most incredibly attractive people she has ever seen.*

If trials are necessary, they used them as the glue to hold their hearts together through it all and they came out closer and stronger than they went in. Jackie still smiles like she did on their wedding day when she talks about their life together and the wonderful love and friendship they shared.

As Jackie puts it, "We would have been happily married for 68 years right now, had he not passed away a few years back. We *are* still married, we just aren't together in this world, but he will always be the love of my life." And their love affair would continue long after his days on this Earth were done.

Sigh... What a beautiful story. I always hoped I would find that kind of history with one partner for my entire life. I dreamed of the day when all my life's experiences were collected into one epic story. It would tell the tale of a man I could trust to love me beyond his own ability, looking past my scars and wrinkles, accepting me *as is,* and still found me irresistible. Not because of any outer beauty, but because of the *'me'* he had come to know building our *Happily Even After* together, one day at a time.

I wanted to believe my life could still one day read like a beautiful love story, but it was reading more like a painful tragedy.

With my fairy tale on hold, I carried the pain of rejection now more than ever. I had heard that it was better to be alone than to be with someone and still feel alone. *Alone* meant pain, but everyone I passed carried private pain. What I endured may not be as difficult as the next, but enduring it challenged me the same.

Pain is no respecter of persons. Scars may come in different shapes and sizes, but all were reminders that what we endured didn't kill us. Pain gives people strength and a fresh perspective. It gave me a deeper compassion for those who were hurting, especially those in my *Happily Even After.*

Life was all so overwhelming. If so many people had failed at finding the fairy tale, how could I assume I would be any different? How did the successful couples do it? Were they just lucky? Did they have a little something different, something special? What was it they possessed that I didn't?

They were both equally far from perfect just like everyone else. What made the difference for them? I was desperate to know their secret, and why had they been keeping it to themselves?

Was it some miraculous gift from God? Was it acts of selflessness? Questions seemed endless, but I desired to follow in their footsteps. It took a whole lot more love than most people were willing to give. It would mean letting go of *self.* Happily Even After wasn't possible for two individuals. It was, however, possible with one very committed "US".

For now I'd live with a smile on the outside until one showed up on the inside. *Fake it 'til you make it,* they say. It didn't matter how desperately I tried to protect my 'superhuman' facade. Breaking down in public is *way* too human and nobody has time for that.

I wanted to be real, but the 'real me' was weak. Many times I sang about the strength of God and my faith in Him. But, I always shared with my friends, "If at the first sign of trouble, you fall apart, then did you really believe what you sang about?" It's okay to be weak but I didn't have to fall apart. I just fell into the arms of Christ.

Jackie made me realize you can always focus on what didn't make you happy, but it's better to focus on what did. They found happiness, not in each other, but in the whole picture, good with the bad. They took seriously, *richer or poorer, in sickness and in health.* Happiness could be lost if it was found in one or the other.

It is *"...**in our weakness, He is made strong.**"*

2 Corinthians 12:9-11

I was not exempt from this truth. Trusting God was easier said than done but losing this battle, however difficult, was not an option, my story depended on it.

I wanted to continue my story but felt I was on endless hold, waiting for Mr. Kind Regards. We were together, but not together. I had a chunk of his heart but not all of it. What good would that do me? I knew I couldn't place my trust in half, even three quarters of a commitment.

I would accept all or nothing. I was stronger now, but I wasn't made of armor, nor was any part of me wearing any, and that made me vulnerable. The fight was draining at times, but I wasn't sure if he was fighting harder for me, or the ghost of fairy tale's past. It was exhausting at times.

I needed to take a slow walk down the path of life and check out the view for a while. That meant putting away my desire to work everything out right now. It felt safer to me to have a plan and watch it play out. I wasn't comfortable with my future in anyone's hands. To be honest, not even God's.

I had heard and read God's promises all my life, hiding them in my heart. But, believing them in the face of adversity was a different story. This would take an active faith I prayed I possessed.

There were lessons with each up and down of the roller coaster of life. I would go back and forth, in and out of fear and just when I felt *I got this,* life would prove me wrong one more time. Happiness wasn't about all those things I was searching for. Happiness would be fleeting anyway.

I wanted to possess it, but what I truly needed was not happiness but Joy. I had a habit of mistaking the two for each other. They look like twins, but happiness was something to look for, like a knight in shining armor, or a glass slipper, even a *Happily Even After.* It's something that can be put on or taken off.

Joy, however, is something you are on the inside. It is not based on circumstances, but on an attitude of the heart. Its source is God, found in His presence. It can't be taken away. It can't be lost. It can only be given away or neglected.

"In His presence, there is fullness of joy." ~ Psalm 16:11

Joy comes with a grateful heart, knowing all I am and all I have is truly a blessing, a gift from God.

"Don't let your happiness depend on something you can lose."

C.S. Lewis

Not Even A Dog Fight

*Julian & Jackie
McKenzie*

Chapter Twenty Three

~ *Life Is A Glorious Gift* ~

Life is so confusing. It brings some of the greatest joys, and greatest sorrows all wrapped up in one strangely glorious gift. If given a choice, would you still choose life? Which one? They are all similar, but with no guarantees. You could be happier than you ever thought possible. You might laugh hysterically at times, creating some amazing memories, but the tears could be as numerous as the stars.

Sleepless nights, betrayals and heartaches might be as the sand on the beach. Sadness could, at times, overshadow any happiness you may experience. It won't kill you though you may think it will. Go ahead. Take one and all its possibilities. Would you still? Life is crazy sometimes but I must say it beats the alternative, even when things don't work out.

I was supposed to be enjoying the one life God had given me and in living it, I would learn to love myself, give more of myself away and experience some of life's greatest adventures. It would require a firm stand in faith, living with joy.

"Only, live your life in a manner worthy of the gospel of Christ, so that, whether I come and see you or am absent and hear about you, I will know that you are standing firm in one spirit, striving side by side with one mind for the faith of the gospel."
Philippians 1:27 ESV

Life truly is a glorious gift, but the gift of life is exactly that, a gift of... life. That's all. Life in itself was not designed to reward me with happiness. It has no power to do so. I alone possess the power within myself to experience happiness or sadness in using the gift, sharing the gift or giving it away. It's more than just a choice. It's an *active* pursuit of that choice.

"Life happens then you die." True enough, but life happens. The time between the sound of the starter's pistol and the finish line is what happens in between, the *dash*, fondly named by some. Short or long, grand or small, ups or downs, life happens.

What was I doing with my dash? That was the question. Life is short and the choice is up to *me*. There was no end to the possibilities if I stopped living life as a victim. I could be victorious because God's love and promises were endless. He was the God of second chances. That alone should fill me with joy.

I witnessed that joy as my son and his wife, LeeAnn, filled their dash with love for each other. Love had dealt her a bad hand the first time around, and to watch her take this journey was a beautiful display of God's grace. I watched as the two embarked on a journey of personal growth, fighting the enemy many long distance relationships endure. It was a second chance for her, and as a military wife, she was asked to sacrifice more than most. She did it with integrity as he served God, her, and his country with honor.

I witnessed it again as my daughter and her fiancé united forces, embracing the pleasure and acceptance of God. Life hadn't favored them either. But, with a second chance at *Happily Even After*, they started their journey with adoring family and friends encircling them. Holding hands, sharing vows, and with that one long awaited kiss they said to the whole world *we are now one flesh*.

It was another beautiful ceremony surrounded by a sea of white lace and chiffon as I had seen many times before. The first wedding, though I was cynical, gave way to healing. The second wedding on the beach birthed a newfound freedom. This time, sadness melted into genuine hope, not only for the two believing and determined lovebirds, but for me too.

My eyes followed the happy couple with a heart overflowing with joy as they walked from the handmade arbor, past the warm glow of the sunset's reflection over the pond. It captured my thoughts as I paused to take it all in. I couldn't help but wonder how this *ready-made* family would handle the adversities to come.

They shared the fire of life and the passion of love, but the struggle the two would face keeping it all together was the real foe to be defeated. I knew their determination declared the struggle would bring them closer to their creator, and to each other.

I was hoping that, if nothing else, my children learned to persevere as my mom had taught me. Trial is inevitable, but in overcoming adversity, they'd see the very nature of God, become stronger and in the midst of it, display their *Happily Even After* for the world to see.

Through all life brings us, "It is through our adversities we come to know our Lord more." ~ Padre Pio.

Now we all share the same *Happily Even After*. It isn't perfect and it never will be, but together we live, together we struggle, together we love and find joy in the most unlikely places. We discovered happiness is a garment to be worn, but true joy is a gift to be cherished. We find it inside our own hearts, nurture it and share it with the world, the glorious gift of life.

"In the presence of God, I intend to find, nurture and share the gift of joy, no glass slipper necessary."

K. Marie

Chapter Twenty Four

~ Conclusion ~

I was out on the beach once again. No weddings this time, just friends and families. Six fishing poles planted in the sand were awaiting grand catches. Frisbees were flying high. Wind surfers holding steady while board surfers eagerly anticipated the next swell. Even paddle boards and canoes joined the celebration the beautiful day offered.

The laughter from the *littles* and the sounds of seagulls crying for bits of day old tortilla chips filled the air. Joggers were jogging, athletes preparing and the *gray hairs* walking hand in hand as they counted more years behind them than ahead.

Bright orange flags waved at each passer-by from atop lifeguard stands, while cautious parents kept a watchful eye on their *tinies.* Confidence came with the occasional drive-by of the Ocean Rescue Team. Cell phones and cameras, hoping to freeze time, focused on life and the living of it all around.

Colorful beach umbrellas dotted the coastline for as far as the eye could see, reminding me of the colorful seasons of our lives. I sat comparing myself to what seemed on the outside like happy lives and wondered how I measured up. I myself had lesser days to count than I'd already counted. Even still, the possibilities ahead of me were as vast as the panoramic view set before me.

Fine clouds brushed the sky. Not even a hint of rain but I knew more ominous clouds were on the way. Approaching weather and the promise of one last pre-Fall thunderstorm were in the forecast. It was one thing we could all count on in life, but that wasn't going to stop me from enjoying right now. I was determined to live it *Happily Even After.*

I now believed someone *could* love me, and never stop loving me until the end. We *would* find each other one-day. It was *my* dream, *my* fairy tale. It was out there and all I had to do was believe. The distance between believing and accomplishing was getting shorter and shorter. But it isn't something to be found or fetched. It isn't the end of the beginning or the beginning of the end.

It is the destined journey between one rather ordinary Prince Charming and one Cinderella Wannabe who seek their very own fairy tale side by side. It is about rebuilding the castle over and over again. It's finding out who each other is and to whom we belong. It is about letting someone love you, not forcing it, keeping the fire, passion and struggle alive, through adversity when it finds you. It is about mutual trust and unconditional love that require sacrifice. It is in the covenant itself.

It's also about the covenant between God and man. It isn't necessarily about finding someone, rather finding joy inside your own heart. It's realizing you aren't broken because your life doesn't match up to the ideal you, or others set for you. You don't need fixing, or tweaking because your life turned out different than you planned, it is profoundly yours and yours alone to live.

Happily Even After is learning to find joy, *even* after great loss, struggle, and a trip through the valley of the shadow of death, knowing that a loving God cares about you.

I may not have found my Prince Charming yet, but I have found joy. You may still be searching for your fairy tale, but if you trust God, it's there you find your *Happily Even After.*

~ Just The Beginning ~

~ My Life Is But A Weaving ~

My life is but a weaving
Between my God and me.
I cannot choose the colors
He weaveth steadily.

Oft times He weaveth sorrow
And I in foolish pride
Forget He sees the upper
And I the underside.

Not till the loom is silent
and the shuttles cease to fly
Will God unroll the canvas
and reveal the reason why.

The dark threads are as needful
In the weaver's skillful hand
As the threads of gold and silver
In the pattern He has planned.

He knows, He loves, He cares
Nothing this truth can dim.
He gives the very best to those
Who leave the choice to Him.

Unknown

~ References ~

Holy Bible ~ English Standard Version

Holy Bible ~ The New American Bible

Marriage For Life ~ Dr. Richard Marks, PHD

Movie Quotes ~

> When Harry Met Sally
>
> About Time
>
> Bull Durham
>
> Under The Tuscan Sun
>
> Runaway Bride
>
> The Holiday
>
> You've Got Mail
>
> Jupiter Ascending

Song References ~

> Disney's Cinderella
>
> Disney's Snow White
>
> Beautiful – Kari Jobe

Quotes~

> Thomas 'a Kempis
>
> Albert Einstein
>
> Padre Pio
>
> C.S. Lewis
>
> Ben Franklin

Online ~

> Wikipedia
>
> Webster's Dictionary

Google

www.ingramcontent.com/pod-product-compliance
Lightning Source LLC
Chambersburg PA
CBHW070804280326
41934CB00012B/3050